VEN. S. M.

Jno. Massengale, between 1860 and 1869. Alto, S. M. Denson, 1911.

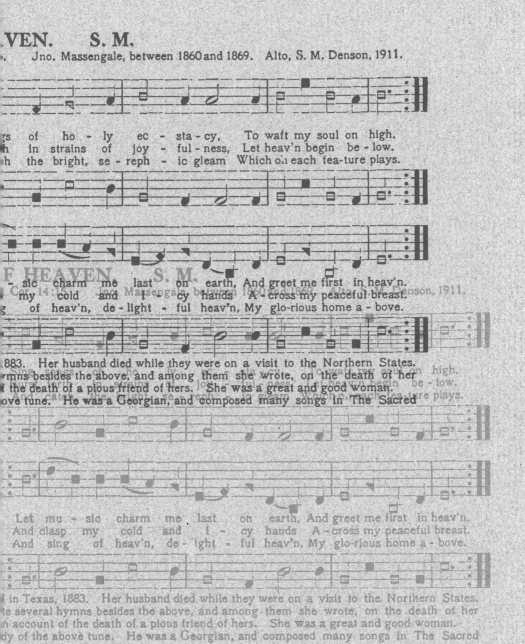

s of ho - ly ec - sta - cy, To waft my soul on high.
h in strains of joy - ful - ness, Let heav'n begin be - low.
h the bright, se - reph - ic gleam Which on each fea - ture plays.

- sic charm me last on earth, And greet me first in heav'n.
my cold and i - cy hands A - cross my peaceful breast.
g of heav'n, de - light - ful heav'n, My glo - rious home a - bove.

883. Her husband died while they were on a visit to the Northern States.
mns besides the above, and among them she wrote, on the death of her
t the death of a pious friend of hers. She was a great and good woman.
ove tune. He was a Georgian, and composed many songs in The Sacred

Let mu - sic charm me last on earth, And greet me first in heav'n.
And clasp my cold and i - cy hands A - cross my peaceful breast.
And sing of heav'n, de - light - ful heav'n, My glo - rious home a - bove.

d in Texas, 1883. Her husband died while they were on a visit to the Northern States.
te several hymns besides the above, and among them she wrote, on the death of her
n account of the death of a pious friend of hers. She was a great and good woman.
dy of the above tune. He was a Georgian, and composed many songs in The Sacred

SING TO ME OF HEAVEN

SING TO ME OF HEAVEN

A Study of Folk and Early American

Materials in Three Old Harp Books

Dorothy D. Horn

UNIVERSITY OF FLORIDA PRESS
GAINESVILLE

1970

A University of Florida Press Book

LIBRARY OF CONGRESS
CATALOG CARD NO. 74-99212
ISBN 0-8130-0293-1

Designed by Stanley D. Harris

PRINTED FOR THE PUBLISHER BY
STORTER PRINTING COMPANY, INCORPORATED
GAINESVILLE, FLORIDA

To

ALLEN IRVINE MCHOSE

A delightful teacher

Preface

THIS BOOK is designed for people who want to know something about Old Harp music. Since presumably these people will be musicians of some sort, a certain basic technical knowledge of music is taken for granted.

It is true that some sections of this book, particularly Chapter VIII, will be of more interest to those who have gone deeper into the science of musical theory. The average reader, if there be such a thing, may wish to skim such sections or to skip them entirely. But it is the hope of the author that all readers will get the general idea that this music is respect-worthy: first, because it is authentic Americana and, second, because it is of intrinsic interest to trained musicologists and theorists. It is, of course, also fun to sing.

A word must be said about the notation used in the musical examples. In general the notation is that of the book from which the example was taken: round notes for the early things, four-shape notation for examples from *The Southern Harmony* and *The Original Sacred Harp,* and seven-shape notation for examples from *The New Harp of Columbia.* If an example occurs in all three of the last named books, the notation is that of the first named reference.

Since each of the three books which form the basis of this study uses a different method of connecting the three or four staves of the score, a simple bar, as used in *The Southern Harmony,* has been employed in all examples, solely to give some semblance of unity. Also, none of the books is consistent in the finer matters of notation. An attempt has been made to copy each example as is, but despite careful proofing an occasional discrepancy may have crept in.

Although two of the books use a scale "fa-sol-la-fa-sol-la-mi-fa," the seven-syllable terminology has been used throughout the text when scale tones are referred to. This is obviously for clarity, since in the seven-syllable system "fa," for instance, refers only to the fourth degree of the scale, whereas in the earlier system it might be either the first or the fourth degree.

As is stated in the text, the material for this book was gathered over a long period of time. As a result, early and rather superficial studies of certain of the problems herein treated have appeared over the years: "Shape-Note Hymnals and the Art Music of Early America," *Southern Folklore Quarterly*, v, 4 (December, 1941); "Dyadic Harmony in the Sacred Harp," *Southern Folklore Quarterly*, ix, 4 (December, 1945); "Folk-Hymn Texts in Three Old Harp Books," *Tennessee Folklore Society Bulletin*, xxii, 4 (December, 1956); and "Tune Detecting in 19th Century Hymnals," *Tennessee Folklore Society Bulletin*, xxvi, 4 (December, 1960). In addition, Chapter viii first appeared as an article in *The Journal of American Folklore* (October–December, 1958), and Chapter vii is based on a paper read before the Southeastern Section of the American Musicological Society in 1961.

Acknowledgments

S O MANY PEOPLE have helped with this book. To begin with, Butler University granted me a Sabbatical leave, during which time I revised, expanded, and verified my earlier notes and gathered materials for chapters VI and XII. A grant from the American Philosophical Society supplied money to do some necessary traveling.

Librarians have been very kind. Besides the anonymous helpers of the Music Division of the New York Public Library and the British Museum Reading Room, I should like to thank Miss Pollyanna Creekmore, chief of the McClung Historical Collection, Lawson McGhee Library, Knoxville; Miss Virginia Turrentine of Maryville College; Mr. Frank P. Grisham of the Religion Section of the Joint University Libraries in Nashville; and Mrs. Ruth Noyes of the Ralph Vaughan Williams Memorial Library in Cecil Sharp House, London, all of whom gave me free use of their stacks and their rare books. In addition, Mr. W. Best Harris, of the Central Reference Library, Plymouth, England, not only allowed me to examine the manuscript collection of the Rev. Sabine Baring-Gould, but also furnished me with information about hotels in Plymouth and a guide book to the city. My thanks also to Mr. B. Damery of the British Museum Copyright Office, who gave invaluable advice about the copyright of the British examples used in this book and also supplied me with publishers' addresses.

Publishers of material I wanted to quote have been very gracious. Mr. Hugh McGraw, secretary of the Sacred Harp Publishing Company, has allowed me to quote at will from the copyrighted material in *The Original Sacred Harp*. Mr. W. E. Critchley, librarian of the Public Library in Aberdeen, Scotland, obtained permission to use "Fair Rosie Ann" by the simple method of phoning Alexander Keith, editor of *Last Leaves of Traditional Ballads and Ballad Airs*, which was printed by a private organization. My thanks to both gentlemen. J. Curwen and Sons granted permission to quote "Just as the Tide was Flowing," as did the Oxford University Press in the matter of "Samuel Young." The University Press of Virginia, which has brought out a 1969 edition of the Davis *Traditional*

Ballads of Virginia, allowed me to quote "The Three Crows." Permission to use the material in Chapter VIII was granted by *The Journal of American Folklore,* which printed the earlier article. All other material quoted appears to be outside the copyright laws, although I am deeply indebted to the Westminster Press, the Oxford University Press, and Holt, Rinehart and Winston, Inc., for help in ascertaining this.

Certain individuals also are due my heartfelt thanks. Mrs. Ralph Vaughan Williams and Miss Maude Karpeles fed me and gave me valuable introductions and advice. Raymond and Joyce Hamrick of Macon, Georgia, had me as a house guest for a week while I examined their microfilm of Ingalls' *Christian Harmony* and their large collection of old singing-school manuals. They also took me to several singings which used *The Sacred Harp.* Joseph Yasser was enthusiastic and encouraging about the section on Dyadic Harmony and helped me to get the American Philosophical Society grant. James Stivers of Butler was invaluable in working out the theories of modality, and many, many of my students at Butler responded to my request for old hymnals and old singing-school books.

Last, but by no means least, thanks to the Old Harpers themselves who welcomed a not very strong alto to their singings and made her feel quite at home.

Contents

I

Knox County Old Harp Singers this Sunday will be with Calvary Baptist Church in Sevier County, on the Wear's Valley Road about three miles from Pigeon Forge. A special bus will leave Knox County Court House at 9:30 a.m. and the singing will start at 10:30. All singers are to take a basket lunch.

The Knoxville (Tennessee) *Journal*
Saturday, September 2, 1967

CRUEROGNO

SUCH NOTICES are, alas, no longer very common. Only a few years ago, if you lived in Kentucky, Tennessee, Georgia, or Alabama, you could find notices similar to the above in the local paper almost any weekend in the spring, summer, or autumn. Should you see such an announcement today by all means follow it up, for you are in for an interesting experience and one far removed from the twentieth century.

The little church will almost certainly be in the country and may equally well be named Cedar Creek, Shiloh, Pleasant Hill, Mt. Lebanon, or Eusebia. There will be modern cars parked in the churchyard: Chevrolets, Fords, Chryslers, Buicks, and probably a bus or two. The people inside will look much like people anywhere, but the majority of them will be middle-aged and elderly folk. The music you will hear goes right back to the beginnings of musical life in America.

At the front of the church chairs will be placed, several rows deep, so that they form a hollow square. On these chairs sit the singers: bass, tenor (which always carries the melody), counter (alto), and tribble (soprano). You will be surprised to see both men and women in every section except the bass. The rest of the church will be filled with listeners, who sometimes join in the singing if they have a book and are not too shy. People wander in and out of the open door, children play around the churchyard, courting couples sit decorously in cars or trade wisecracks around the church steps. It is a happy and relaxed atmosphere.

Each singing has a chairman. This is a man with a good loud voice who must have two further qualifications: he must know everyone for

1

miles around, and he must know every song in the book by its page number. The chairman calls on the leaders, each of whom comes to the center of the square to lead one tune.

"There's Brother Walls, from over at Tallassee," the chairman may say. "Come right up here, Brother Walls. What are you going to lead for us today?"

There are usually a few introductory remarks as the leader rises and comes forward, particularly if Brother Walls is elderly. He may be deprecatory ("Well now, my throat's been pretty bad this morning") or inspirational ("Folks, there's a fine message in this here song"). He gives the number of his chosen song, and the chairman nods happily.

"Number sixteen," he echoes. "That's old Greenfields; that's a good old song. You sing it, brothers and sisters. Give us the pitch, Brother Walls."

Brother Walls does so, sometimes with the aid of a pitch pipe or tuning fork, but sometimes without. In the latter case, the pitch is frequently the written one; these are musical people and many have pitch recognition. Almost never does the pitch vary by more than a half step unless the tune is consciously pitched low for easier singing.

"Sol–mi–do–mi–sol," bellows Brother Walls in a clear and powerful tenor. (This is a seven-shape singing.) "Sound your pitches!"

He makes a sweeping gesture toward the singers, who respond by singing the starting pitch in each part. Then they are off on the tune itself, first with syllables, then, the second time round, with words. The singing is loud and enthusiastic and is accompanied by encouraging remarks from the chairman, energetic arm-waving by the leader, and spirited foot-tapping by many people in the church.

If there is dinner-on-the-grounds, there is a break for the good country basket dinner at twelve. In the afternoon the singing begins again and goes on until three-thirty or four; then, after a benediction, the members of the host church are thanked and everyone piles into the cars and buses and goes home.

The books used by the singers vary in different sections of the country, but they are remarkably alike. They are oblong books, written in open score for three or four voices, they open at the side, and they are printed in shaped notes. Some books use a seven-shape notation, and some use the older four-shape.

And now has come the time to talk a little about the background of Old Harp singing and how it evolved into its present form. The following explanation is admittedly oversimplified; this history would make a book in itself. A far better idea may be obtained from the early chapters of Gilbert Chase's *America's Music*, a book to be found in most public libraries.[1]

During the second half of the eighteenth century a favorite social diversion in New England was the singing school. Singing schools seem to have begun in an attempt to improve the singing in church, but they also provided a welcome and acceptable social outlet. A master was hired who taught people to read music and to sing at sight, and the books these singers used looked very much like the Old Harp books of today except that they were printed in round notes. They contained psalm and hymn tunes, anthems and fuguing pieces, and our earliest American composers were kept busy by the demand for new material. These composers were singing school masters themselves, and we should pause to say a little about them.

They were, first of all, typical Yankee jacks-of-all-trades. Supply Belcher, compiler of *The Harmony of Maine*, was a schoolteacher, tavern keeper, and local politician. Justin Morgan, who published no book of his own but who contributed to many, bred horses and was town clerk. Amariah Hall farmed, kept an inn, and sold straw bonnets; Oliver Holden, responsible for four books to be mentioned later, served in the armed forces of the Revolution, then turned his attention to real estate, Masonry, storekeeping, politics, and, of course, music. William Billings, the greatest of them all, was a tanner by trade. All of these men, and many more like them, had an intense love of music that transcended a considerable ignorance of its conventional technical aspects.

For these men were largely self-taught. Perhaps they had studied the "Introduction to Practical Music" in William Tans'ur's *Compleat Harmony*, published in London in 1736 and popular in the colonies, but this was principally a set of rules for voice leading and must have been largely unintelligible to its American readers. Mostly these early composers seem to have learned from attending singing schools themselves, from the study of such European music as came their way, and by a trial-and-error method. The results were to horrify Lowell Mason a half century later: "The style derived from Tans'ur and other inferior English composers spread widely, superseding in great measure the admirable old 'Church Tunes' [i.e.: the English and Scottish psalm tunes] and preparing the way for the still lower character of tunes which came up

1. Chapters 1, 2, 3, 7, 10, 11.

at about the time of the American Revolution, and which are even now heard in some parts of the country."[2]

This opinion, parenthetically, was that held by most musicians up to about the nineteen-thirties. Thanks to the work of Dr. George Pullen Jackson, to a rising school of American musicologists, and to Dr. Howard Hanson's interest in all American music, the genuine, though untutored, musical ability evident in this early music began to be appreciated.

New England compositions were of three types, all of which may be found in Old Harp books today.

Hymn tunes are usually in one of the standard meters (Long, Common, or Short), and have four phrases, frequently with a modulation to the dominant in the middle. Each is designed to be used with a variety of rhymed texts in the same meter. These texts are frequently metrical versions of the psalms.

Anthems are long sectional compositions, somewhat contrapuntal in character. They frequently have unrhymed Scriptural texts.

Fuguing pieces begin in four-part harmony and come to a cadence after two, occasionally four, phrases. Then each voice enters alone, somewhat in the manner of a round, after which all voices come together in a strong cadence at the end. The text is rhymed and is usually in one of the hymn meters.[3]

In the last years of the eighteenth century the singing schools and their music began to fall into disfavor in the larger towns and cities. As Chase says, "But they [the singing schools and their music] lived on chiefly in the hinterlands, gradually ousted from the dominant urban centers by the pressure of progress and the imposition of more sophisticated standards."[4] These hinterlands were the backwoods sections of the North, Southeast, and West. In the last case, the singing schools seem to have followed the rapidly advancing frontier. From Cincinnati the movement tended to turn south and to spread out through Kentucky and Tennessee, where it was reinforced by the westward migration of such masters as had come south through Virginia and North Carolina.[5] This tradition lingered on in the rural sections of the Southeast until well into the twentieth century, and today's Old Harp singings are what remains of it.

2. *The National Psalmist,* Preface.
3. For a much fuller discussion of the above, see *The Church Music of William Billings* by J. Murray Barbour.
4. Page 145.
5. Charles Hamm, "The Chapins and Sacred Music in the South and West."

Two things happened right about the time that the singing schools declined in popularity in New England. The first was that Yankee ingenuity devised a way to simplify the teaching of sight-singing. This was by printing the music in shaped notes, one shape for each syllable of the solmization used. It is an open question as to whether the credit for this idea should go to Andrew Law, whose *Art of Singing*, published at Cambridge, was in its fourth edition in 1803, or to the partnership of William Little and William Smith, whose *Easy Instructor,* printed at Albany, is dated 1802 but was probably copyrighted four years earlier.[6]

Both books used the four-syllable system of solmization, for the seven-syllable system, so common now, was then unknown in this country. Law's book was printed without staves; the Little and Smith book uses the conventional open score, and it is their system that influenced subsequent shape-note publishing.

Since the four-syllable system of solmization is still very much in use in Old Harp circles and has considerable antiquarian interest, it should perhaps be explained. The following is condensed from Thomas Morley's *A Plaine and Easie Introduction to Pracktical Musick,* published in London in 1597, the first part of which is instructions in sight-singing.

The method of naming the various pitches in the vocal range is derived from the Guidonian hexachord system, as in Ex. 1.

Ex. 1

This scheme, Morley makes clear, could be continued up or down indefinitely, for as Master Gnorius tells his pupil Philomathes:

Phil: Be these the only wayes you may have these notes in the whole Gam?
Master: These and their eights: as what is done in Gam ut may also be done in G sol–re–ut and likewise G sol–re–ut in alt.

6. Frank J. Metcalf, "The Easy Instructor."

And a little later:

> Master: Whereas you say there is nothing beneath Gam ut you deceive yourself. For musicke is included in no certain bounds. . . . And therefore call to minde that which I told you concerning the keyes and their eights; for if mathematically you consider it, it is true as well without the compasse of the scale as within: and so may be continued indefinitely.

With all this in mind, it can be seen that the following table of syllables would result:

G   could be sol, re, or ut, depending on the hexachord.
A   could be re, la, or mi.
B♭   could only be fa.
B   could only be mi.
C   could be fa, ut, or sol.
D   could be sol, re, or la.
E   could be mi or la.
F   could be fa or ut.

Summing this up, a hexachord could start only on G, C, or F; and the syllable "ut" could occur only on these three tones. B is the only tone that has two forms; in order to keep the half-step between the third and fourth tones of the hexachord it must be B flat in the F hexachord and B natural in the G hexachord.

Since "ut" could be used only once in any hexachord and only for the lowest note in that hexachord, the syllables from the next highest hexachord would have to be used to fill out the octave. Thus the octave with F as "ut" would have to be sung with the syllables shown in Ex. 2.

Ex. 2

ut   re   mi   fa   sol   la   mi   fa

Ex. 3

fa   sol   la   fa   sol   la   mi   fa

Ex. 4

Fa   Sol   La   Fa   Sol   La   Me   Fa

Ex. 5

Do   Ra   Mi   Fa   Sol   La   Si   Do

But this has the ridiculous result of F and its "eight" having different syllables, so the lowest three notes are given their names in the next lowest hexachord, which results in the syllables shown in Ex. 3. A glance at the hexachord chart will show that this system works equally well on C; this, of course, would satisfy the requirements of sixteenth-century music. In *The Original Sacred Harp,* one of the three books used in this study, the Morley scale with the Little and Smith shapes appears in the explanation of the rudiments of music as shown in Ex. 4.

The system as used in the shape-note books is, of course, transposable to all keys; but, as far as the author knows, the four-syllable solmization survives today only in these books.

The Masons, Lowell and Timothy B., were undoubtedly responsible for introducing the seven-syllable solmization to the shape-note books, even though they themselves deplored such musical crudity.[7] The "Introduction to Music" of the Masons' *Ohio Sacred Harp* has this to say about the proper method:[8]

> The most correct method of solmization is to apply a distinct syllable to each note of the scale, viz: the syllable DO to *one,* RE (ray) to *two,* MI to *three,* FA to *four,* SOL to *five,* LA to *six,* and SI (see) to *seven.* Indeed, by pursuing the common method of only *four* syllables, singers are almost always superficial. It is therefore recommended to all who wish to be thorough, to pursue the system of seven syllables, disregarding the different forms of the notes.

Despite this last sentence, shapes were applied in a seven-syllable system in some of Mason's own books.[9] Curiously enough, most seven-shape notations retain the Little and Smith shapes for fa, sol, la, and mi. Thus the syllables and shapes used in *The New Harp of Columbia,* the only seven-shape book used in this study, are shown in Ex. 5.

The most obvious advantage of a shape-note notation is that it dispenses with the whole wearisome business of learning key signatures, thus removing one hurdle in the teaching of sight-singing. Obviously, if one knows the shape for the keynote, a signature is unnecessary. Many tunes in *The New Harp of Columbia* are entirely without signature.[10]

This shortcut to sight-singing has one limiting factor. Shapes have never been devised for chromatic inflections; in consequence, modula-

---

7. George Pullen Jackson, *White Spirituals in the Southern Uplands,* p. 18.
8. *Ibid.,* quoted on p. 17.
9. *Ibid.,* p. 18.
10. See NH, pp. 24, 26, 27, and 29, for examples.

tions, altered chords, and the harmonic and melodic forms of the minor are impossible. The singers don't mind, and the music doesn't seem to suffer much.

The second thing that happened to the singing school manuals around 1800 was that they began to contain folk hymns. The earliest of these had probably arisen spontaneously sixty or seventy years before in the revivals of the Great Awakening inaugurated by Jonathan Edwards in 1734 and continued by George Whitefield, the English Methodist. Occasionally one of these tunes was printed (the tune "Fairfield," for instance, had been included in Oliver Holden's *Union Harmony* of 1793), but mostly these were communicated orally. *The Christian Harmony*, compiled by Jeremiah Ingalls and published in Exeter, New Hampshire, in 1805, was the first singing school manual to print these tunes in any great number.

What Sweet calls "the frontier phase of the Second Awakening" began in 1800 with the famous camp meeting in Logan County, Kentucky, and from this time on the camp meeting seems to have been a tremendous generator of religious folk song.[11] The more popular of these songs seem to have spread through the country with a speed comparable only to that with which the latest dirty story spreads through the undergraduate collegiate population of today.

Thus it was that the shape-note books of the southeast, from *The Kentucky Harmony* of Ananias Davisson in 1815 to the 1936 and the 1960 revisions of *The Original Sacred Harp*, contain many folk hymns.[12] As time went by, other tunes were added by processes which will be explained in subsequent chapters.

The music of the Old Harps was largely ignored by scholars until 1933, when the late George Pullen Jackson brought out his *White Spirituals in the Southern Uplands*. Dr. Jackson was a professor at Vanderbilt University, and, though music was not his teaching subject, he was a dedicated investigator in the field of folk hymnody. *Spiritual Folk-Songs of Early America* came out in 1937, followed by *Down East Spirituals and Others* in 1943 and *Another Sheaf of White Spirituals* in 1952. Though Dr. Jackson wrote other books in related fields, these four books are classics and are musts for anyone who professes an interest in religious folk song.

11. William Warren Sweet, *Religion in the Development of American Culture*, p. 148.
12. The author uses the term "folk hymn" rather loosely here; wait till Chapter III for explanations.

This study is based on the material to be found in three Old Harp books still in use today. The earliest of these is William Walker's *Southern Harmony and Musical Companion,* written mostly in three parts and in the four-shape notation. The first edition came out in 1835 and was printed in New Haven, Connecticut, although subsequent editions were printed in Philadelphia. The last edition is that of 1854. A reprint of this edition, sponsored by the Young Men's Progress Club of Benton, Kentucky, was published by Hastings House of New York in 1939. *The Southern Harmony* is still in use around Benton.

Much of the material of *The Southern Harmony* appears in *The Sacred Harp,* a manual compiled by Walker's brother-in-law Benjamin Franklin White, assisted by E. J. King, in 1844. There have been many editions and revisions of this famous book. The two latest, very much in use today, are the Denson revisions of 1936 and of 1960; these are alike as far as basic material goes and form the second of the books chosen for this study.[13] Both Denson revisions are called *The Original Sacred Harp.* Whether the 1936 or the 1960 revision is used, *The Original Sacred Harp* is undoubtedly the most widely used manual in the South today. It uses a four-shape notation.

The third book is *The New Harp of Columbia,* a seven-shape manual in four parts. Its compiler was Marcus Lafayette Swan. Although the date on the title page is 1921, the plates, owned by the Methodist Episcopal Church, have not been changed since 1867.[14] As its name implies, *The New Harp* is a revision of an older *Harp of Columbia.* This was published in 1849 in Knoxville. *The New Harp of Columbia* is used almost exclusively in East Tennessee today.

People wonder sometimes why shape-note singers call themselves "Old Harp Singers" since no instrumental accompaniment, harp or otherwise, is used. In the heyday of the southern singing schools there were, besides *The Harp of Columbia* and *The Sacred Harp,* many other such titles: *The Harp of the South, The Social Harp,* and *The Hesperian Harp,* to mention only a few. Very well, then. These books are old, the word *Harp* is a part of the title, and so those who sing from them are Old Harp Singers.

It is as simple as that.

13. As this goes to press, I understand that another revision is being made.
14. Jackson, *White Spirituals,* p. 327. There was a rumor during the last war that these had been melted down for scrap.

II

The Southern Harmony and Musical Companion, containing a choice collection of Tunes, Hymns, Psalms, Odes, and Anthems, selected from the most eminent authors in the United States, together with nearly one hundred new tunes, which have never been published. . . .

William Walker

T HE ABOVE, taken from the title page of Walker's *Southern Harmony,* gives a very good hint as to how the average singing school manual was compiled. In other words, one lifted the most popular works from older books and added enough new material to make the volume different from its predecessors. This new material was usually of two types: original compositions by one's self or one's friends, and favorite hymns from the hymnals of established denominations. It must be emphasized that the singing school manuals were not designed to be used in church services.

By the middle of the nineteenth century the average singing school manual contained (1) a few psalm tunes of English or Scottish origin, (2) a goodly selection of hymn tunes, fuguing pieces, and anthems by New England composers born in the eighteenth century, (3) a lot of folk hymns (of which more later), and (4) hymns by Lowell Mason and his English and American contemporaries. There are also apt to be a few things not classifiable under any of the above headings, and some of these will be mentioned later.

The three manuals chosen for examination are quite typical. All three contain the psalm tune "Old Hundred" which came to England by way of the Huguenot Psalter of 1551, where the tune was used for the 134th Psalm. *The Southern Harmony* and *The Original Sacred Harp* include "Aylesbury," which the historical edition of *Hymns Ancient and Modern* says is first found in the Cheltham *Book of Psalmody* of 1818.[1] "Dundee" occurs only in *The New Harp.* According to McCutcheon it comes from

1. London, 1932, hymn 449.

the Scottish Psalter of 1615 and was called "French Tune."[2] In Ravenscroft's *Psalmes* of 1621 it is called "Dundee," probably after the town known as the Scottish Geneva. "Devises," also in *The New Harp*, is an English psalm tune of 1810. "Cambridge," in *The Original Sacred Harp*, is another English tune by Dr. John Randall, who lived between 1715 and 1799. The tune certainly appeared in this country as early as 1814.[3]

The most puzzling of these early foreign tunes is that called "Dublin," which is contained in both *The Southern Harmony* and *The New Harp*. In this country it appears as early as 1761 in Lyon's *Urania*, but under the name of "Coleshill." Now "Dublin" (or "Coleshill") bears a very close resemblance to the English psalm tune "Windsor," one of the thirteen tunes printed in the 1698 edition of *The Bay Psalm Book*. Others have noted the similarity: in Dyer's *Philadelphia Selection of Sacred Music* the melody of "Coleshill" is printed above that of "Windsor" with the note "Bass, tenor and alto the same as Windsor." Both versions of the tune are known in the British Isles. The "Windsor" form occurs in the Este Psalter of 1592, while "Dublin Tune" may be found in Thomas Smith's edition (1698) of Simmons' *The Book of Psalms in Metre*.

There are far more Early American works in the three books. And what is an Early American work? The author used the following working definition: a hymn tune, fuguing piece, or anthem whose composer is definitely known and is definitely known to have been born in the eighteenth century. The following list resulted:

1. All Saints New, OSH 444. (All OSH numbers apply to both revisions.) It is here attributed to "Amrick Hall, 1811." This is the Amariah Hall mentioned in Chapter I. It may be found in *The Psalmodist's Companion* of 1793. Fuguing piece.
2. America, SH 27, OSH 36. In both books it is attributed to "Whitmore" and OSH adds "1832." However, it is to be found in Benham's *Social Harmony* of 1798 where it is attributed to "Wetmore." Fuguing piece.
3. Amherst, SH 330, attributed to Billings. It also is in *The Beauties of Harmony*, 1814, and in this, as in all later books, Billings is given as the composer. Fuguing piece.
4. Amity, SH 282, no composer given. It is in *The Psalmodist's Companion* and *The Beauties of Harmony* where it is attributed to "Reed" [Daniel Read]. Fuguing piece.
5. Ballstown, SH 162, OSH 217, NH 161. This popular fuguing piece

2. Robert Guy McCutcheon, *Hymn Tune Names.*
3. It appears in Freeman Lewis' *Beauties of Harmony.*

is usually attributed to Nehemiah Shumway. It may be found in *The Musical Instructor* of 1818.

6. Bridgewater, OSH 276. Attributed to "Lewis Edson, 1782." Confirmed by Metcalf in *The Stories of Hymn Tunes*.[4] Fuguing piece.

7. Calvary, OSH 300. Attributed to "Daniel Read, 1806." It is found earlier than this in *The Psalmodist's Companion*. Fuguing piece.

8. China, SH 276, NH 39. It is by Timothy Swan and may be found in his *New England Harmony*, 1801. Hymn tune in C.M.

9. Claremont (or Cleremont), SH 183, NH 211, OSH 245. This is to be found in Holden's *Worcester Harmony* of 1803. Anthem. It is usually attributed to Jacob Kimball.

10. Concord, OSH 313. OSH attributes it to "Oliver Holden, 1793." It is to be found in that composer's *Union Harmony* of 1793 and marked "never before published." Semi-fuguing piece.

11. Coronation, SH 299, NH 117, OSH 63. The latter attributes it to "Oliver Holden, 1793." This too is in the *Union Harmony* and is marked "published for the first time." Hymn tune in C.M.

12. Cowper, OSH 168. No composer given. It is probably by Oliver Holden, and is attributed to him both by Freeman Lewis and John Wyeth. It may be found in *The Beauties of Harmony*. Fuguing piece.

13. Creation, NH 157. NH attributes this to "Shumway" as do many other books in which this occurs. This, of course, is the Nehemiah Shumway mentioned before, who published his *American Harmony* in 1793. It is included in Holden's *Worcester Harmony*, 1803. Fuguing piece.

14. David's Lamentation, SH 213, OSH 268. The latter attributes this to "William Billings, about 1800." It is in Billings' *Singing Master's Assistant*, 1778. Anthem.

15. Delight, SH 167, OSH 216. In the latter it is attributed to "Coan Guilford about 1800." It is to be found in *The Beauties of Harmony* where the composer is given simply as "Coan." Fuguing piece.

16. Easter Anthem, SH 189, NH 195, OSH 236. This very popular anthem is always attributed to Billings and is to be found in his *Suffolk Harmony* of 1786. Both OSH and Butterworth-Brown place the composition a year earlier.[5]

17. Egypt; NH 150 attributes this to "Swan," but the composer is definitely Timothy Swan and not the compiler of *The New Harp*. It may be found in Swan's *New England Harmony* of 1801. Hymn tune, in 8's instead of one of the church meters.

4. Page 107.

5. Hezekiah Butterworth and Theron Brown, *The Story of the Hymns and Tunes*, p. 475.

18. Enfield, OSH 184. It is here attributed to "S. Chandler, about 1830," but it is to be found both in *The Psalmodist's Companion* and Holden's *Union Harmony*. In the latter the composer is given as "Chandler." Anthem.

19. Exhortation, NH 155, OSH 272. The latter ascribes it to "Doolittle," probably Amos Doolittle (1754–1832). It is found in Jenks' *New England Harmonist* of 1799. Fuguing piece.

20. Farewell Anthem, SH 214, NH 219, OSH 260. No composer is given in any book examined by the author, but it is found as early as 1793 in *The Psalmodist's Companion*.

21. Funeral Anthem, SH 187, OSH 320. This is by Billings and is always ascribed to him. It may be found in *The Beauties of Harmony*.

22. Greenfield, SH 121. This is to be found in Oliver Brownson's *Select Harmony* of 1783 and is by Lewis Edson. Fuguing piece.

23. Greenwich, OSH 183. It is attributed to "Daniel Reed, 1793." ·It is generally attributed to Read except in Caldwell's *Union Harmony* of 1837 where, probably by a misprint, the composer is given as "Mead." It is certainly found as early as 1793, for it is found both in *The Psalmodist's Companion* and Holden's *Union Harmony* of that year. Fuguing piece.

24. Heavenly Vision, SH 206, OSH 250. In both of these the anthem is attributed to Billings, but in both *The Beauties of Harmony* and *The Sacred Melodeon* of 1849, it is attributed to "French," probably the Jacob French of *The Psalmodist's Companion*. The work does not appear in this book. The author found it no earlier than 1814, in *The Beauties of Harmony*.

25. Huntingdon, NH 175, SH 169, OSH 193. This is one of the most popular fuguing pieces, and, when a composer is given, it is always attributed to [Justin] Morgan. It is to be found in Atwill's *New York Collection* of 1794.

26. Invitation, NH 178, OSH 327. In the latter the composer is given as "Jacob Kimboll, 1793." This is the Jacob Kimball, jr., whose *Rural Harmony* was published in 1793. "Invitation" appears on page 29. Fuguing piece.

27. Jubilee, SH 118, OSH 144. In the latter the composer is given as "Oliver Bronson, 1783." This is the Oliver Brownson who compiled *The Select Harmony* of 1783 which contains this tune. Fuguing piece.

28. Lenox, SH 77, NH 42, OSH 40. This is another popular fuguing piece and is always attributed to [Lewis] Edson. OSH gives the date as 1785, but the author found the piece copied by hand on the flyleaf of Tans'ur's *American Harmony* in the Sibley Library

of the Eastman School of Music. The inscription was "Lennex—Ezekiel Allen's Book, 1773." The piece occurs in Holden's *Union Harmony* twenty years later and thereafter in practically every singing school manual.

29. Liberty, SH 68, NH 98, OSH 137. In the latter it is attributed to "Stephen Jenks, 1803." It is to be found, however, in Jenks' *Musical Harmonist* of 1800. Fuguing piece.

30. Lisbon, SH 154, has only the "theme" of the original fuguing piece by Daniel Read, which may be found in his *Columbian Harmonist* of 1806. It was composed earlier, for it appears in the *Union Harmony* of 1793.

31. Majesty, OSH 291. Here it is attributed to "Wm. Billings, 1785." It dates from an earlier time than this, for it is included in Billings' *Singing Master's Assistant* of 1778. Unconventional fuguing piece.

32. Masonic Ode, OSH 228. Though no composer is given, this is by Daniel Belknap and is included in his *Evangelical Harmony* of 1800.

33. Mear, SH 24, NH 14, OSH 49. There is some doubt that this psalm tune really originated in America. John Tasker Howard thought that it might well have been among the first American compositions.[6] According to William Arms Fisher the tune first appeared in Tate and Brady's *New Version of the Psalms of David* in 1755.[7] OSH attributes it to "Aaron Williams, 1760." The author first found it in Lyons' *Urania*, 1761.

34. Middletown, NH 173, with no composer given. Elsewhere it is sometimes spelled "Middleton" and is usually attributed to "Ball" or "Bull." It is possible that this might be the Amos Bull who compiled *The Responsary* in 1795, though this semi-anthem does not appear in it. It does appear in Shumway's *American Harmony* of 1793, where it is attributed to Bull.

35. Milford, NH 152, OSH 273. The latter ascribes it to "James Stephenson, about 1802." This is a charming little Christmas anthem with fuguing elements and is usually attributed to Stephenson. It is to be found in *The American Harmony* of 1793.

36. Montgomery, NH 158. Though NH attributes this to "More," it is actually by Justin Morgan. It appears in both *The Psalmodist's Companion* and *The Union Harmony* of 1793. Fuguing piece.

37. Mount Pleasant, OSH 218. Here it is attributed to "James Leach, 1789"; in *The Beauties of Harmony* the composer is given as "Deolph." It is to be found in Shumway's *American Harmony* of 1793.

38. Newburgh, SH 296, OSH 182. In the latter it is attributed to

6. *Our American Music*, pp. 44–49.
7. *Ye Olde New England Psalm Tunes*, p. 4.

"R. D. Munson, 1810," but it appears four years earlier in Read's *Columbian Harmonist*. Fuguing piece.

39. New Jerusalem, OSH 299. OSH attributes this to "Jeremiah Ingalls, 1804." It appears in *The Beauties of Harmony* (and many later books) with Ingalls given as the composer. Fuguing piece.

40. Ninety-fifth, SH 7, NH 25, OSH 36. In the OSH it is attributed to "Coulton," but in NH the composer is given as "Chapin." The earliest appearance of this fuguing piece found by the author was in *The Beauties of Harmony*, where it is attributed to "Colton."

41. Ninety-third, SH 7, NH 25, OSH 31. This hymn tune in S.M. is really an early folk hymn and has a Jackson reference. It is almost certainly by one of the Chapins; it is attributed to L[ucius] Chapin in *The Beauties of Harmony*. Lucius Chapin fought in the Revolution, later taught singing school in New England, and eventually moved to the Shenandoah Valley in 1787.[8]

42. Northfield, SH 283, NH 115, OSH 155. This is by Jeremiah Ingalls and is in his *Christian Harmony* of 1805. Fuguing piece.

43. Ocean, SH 180, NH 159, OSH 222. This is by Timothy Swan and was first found by the author in Law's *Rudiments of Music*, 1792. Modified fuguing piece.

44. Ode on Science, SH 210, NH 208, OSH 242. In the latter the composer is given as "Deacon Janaziah, 1798." According to Butterworth-Brown, this was composed by Janaziah Summers of Taunton, Massachusetts, for the semicentennial of Stephen Daggett's Academy in 1798.[9] Anthem.

45. Rose of Sharon, SH 200, NH 199, OSH 254. This is by William Billings and is included in his *Singing Master's Assistant*, 1778. OSH gives the date as "about 1793." Anthem.

46. Russia, OSH 107. The composer is given as "Daniel Reed, 1793." It certainly appears in three books of this date: the French *Psalmodist's Companion*, Holden's *Union Harmony*, and Shumway's *American Harmony*. It is in Read's *Columbian Harmonist* of 1806. Fuguing piece.

47. Sherburne, OSH 186. This is attributed to "Daniel Reed, 1793," but it appears in Read's *American Singing Book* in 1785. This is the first American setting of "While Shepherds Watched Their Flocks by Night" and is a fuguing piece.

48. Spring, NH 170, OSH 188. No composer is given, but it appears in Fobes' *Delaware Harmony* of 1809. This anthem is not as popular as some others; the author found it subsequently only in *The American or Union Harmonist* (1831) with no composer given,

8. Hamm, "The Chapins."
9. Pages 330–31.

and in the *Supplement to the Kentucky Harmony* (1825) marked "unknown."

49. Stafford, OSH 78, is attributed to "Daniel Reed, 1793." It is included in *The Psalmodist's Companion* of 1793. Fuguing piece.

50. Suffield, SH 31. This hymn tune in C.M. has no composer given, but in *The Beauties of Harmony, The Christian Harmony* (1841), and *The Sacred Melodeon* (1849), the composer is given as "King." The tune appears in Adgate's *Rudiments of Music,* 1803.

51. Sutton, NH 113. The name of the composer in NH is blurred, but in *The Beauties of Harmony* it is given as "Goff." This fuguing piece appears in *The Psalmodist's Companion.*

52. Symphony, OSH 151. The composer is given as "R. D. Munson, 1810," but this hymn tune in Peculiar Meter appears as early as 1798 in Asahel Benham's *Social Harmony.* It is attributed to Morgan here and in the *Union Harmony* of Caldwell.

53. Virginia, OSH 191. It is here attributed to "Oliver Bronson, 1783." It is to be found in the Adgate-Spicer *Philadelphia Harmony* of 1790. Hymn tune in C.M.

54. Windham, SH 48, NH 18, OSH 38. NH gives the composer as "Leed," SH as "Read," and OSH as "Daniel Read, 1785." It occurs in Read's *American Singing Book* of that year. Hymn tune in L.M.

55. Winter, SH 293, NH 101, OSH 38. Both SH and OSH attribute this to Read. It occurs in his *American Singing Book* (1785) and his *Columbian Harmonist* (1806). It is a hymn tune in C.M.

56. Yarmouth, NH 154. This is attributed to Kimball in Holden's *Worcester Collection* of 1786. Fuguing piece.

There are a few doubtful numbers. "Schenectady," OSH 192, is attributed to Nehemiah Shumway, but the author has been unable to find it in the older manuals. "Sardinia," SH 126, OSH 296, is traditionally supposed to have been composed by an Italian, one G. Gastil. "Whitestown," SH 135, NH 180, ascribed to "Ward," is not found before *The Musical Instructor* of 1818 and is elsewhere attributed to "Howell." And so on.

It should be emphasized that the above list in no way attempts to give the first printing of any of these tunes, except, of course, in the case of the two Holden pieces vouched for by the composer himself. Rather it attempts to isolate a representative body of material dating from an older harmonic tradition that may be used for comparison with the folk hymns in a later chapter.

That brings us to a consideration of the folk hymns in the next chapter of this study.

III

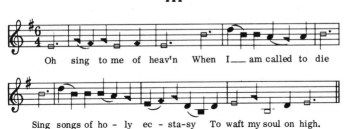

"Sing to Me of Heaven"
Original Sacred Harp, p. 312

"S ING TO ME OF HEAVEN" is a folk hymn. George Pullen Jackson discusses it in *Down East Spirituals and Others*, no. 205, and finds it related to a secular English folk tune called "Sprig of Thyme." The words are by Mrs. Mary Stanley Bunce Dana, afterward Mrs. Shindler, and date from 1840. They were very popular, and not only among rural singers, in the nineteenth century.[1]

What is a folk hymn?

Irving Lowens says that it is ". . . a secular folk tune which happens to be sung to a religious text."[2] Dr. Jackson never really committed himself to a definition, but hints may be found by a careful reading of his books.

For instance, the composer John Powell, in the preface that he wrote for Jackson's *Spiritual Folk-Songs*, offers two hints: first, "The ancestors of the bearers of the Southern tradition of folk music began in very ancient times the practice of singing religious songs to folk tunes" (p. vii). This is of, course, essentially the Lowens idea, and it is by no means new. Many of the Lutheran chorales were set to secular tunes. Further, he writes, "Music lovers were astonished to learn of the existence of these old books [the shape-note manuals] containing a wealth of uniquely beautiful hymn tunes, largely folk tunes and *others composed in the*

1. Butterworth-Brown, p. 228.
2. "John Wyeth's *Repository of Sacred Music*, Part Second: a Northern Precursor of Southern Folk Hymnody."

same idiom" (p. ix). The italics are this author's. Again, Dr. Jackson himself says in the Introduction to the same book, "Among these tunes [the
spiritual songs] my finding of secular analogies was limited usually to
melodic parts instead of whole tunes" (p. 19).

A folk hymn would seem therefore to be (a) a contrafactum of a
secular folk tune, (b) an original tune composed in the idiom of secular
folk music, or (c) a tune patched together, either wholly or in part,
from pre-existent melodic fragments, a process known to musicologists
as centonization.

Dr. Jackson covered the first of these types rather thoroughly; the
second type will be referred to from time to time, and a complete chapter will be devoted to the subject of centonization. But right now, let us
consider a question raised by Mr. Powell's words above: what is the
"idiom" of secular folk music?

First, it must be remembered that Dr. Jackson was concerned only
with tunes; harmony had no interest for him. So "idiom" really means
"melodic idiom." Second, in the opinion of this writer, the melodic idiom
of folk music can never be ascertained, for the simple reason that true
folk music, handed down by oral tradition, is always changing. By the
time folklorists get around to recording it, it has become what Apel
calls "civilized folk song."[3] On the other hand, the musical idiom of the
folk hymn can at least be groped for, since, though these were originally
handed down by oral tradition, the oldest of them have been in print
since the early 1800s.

The procedure was simple enough. A list was made of all tunes occurring in *The Original Sacred Harp*, *The New Harp of Columbia*, and
The Southern Harmony that were also included in Jackson's *Spiritual
Folk-Songs*, *Down East Spirituals*, or *Another Sheaf of White Spirituals*.
These tunes, taken rather empirically as bona fide folk hymns, were
studied as to scales employed, metric and rhythmic characteristics,
and formal and structural characteristics. There are 286 tunes present
in the three manuals that are included by Jackson in his three books. It
is only fair to add that the author disagrees with Jackson about some of
these: "Benevento" (AnS 68), for instance, "China" (DeS 112), or
"America" (DeS 187), for none of which Jackson found folk song backgrounds.[4] However, this group forms a body of material of sufficient

3. *The Harvard Dictionary of Music*, p. 275.
4. "Benevento" is by Samuel Webbe (1740–1816) and according to *The Music
of the Methodist Hymn Book* was originally part of a mass, with the words "Tantum
ergo sacrementum."

scope and backed by sufficient authority to work with. One must begin somewhere.

To begin, 232 of the tunes use some form of gapped scale, either pentatonic or hexatonic. Of the remaining seven-tone melodies several are recognizable contrafacti of pre-existent tunes, some of which are by no means English folk tunes. "Weeping Saviour" (OSH 310) is an oral-tradition version of Bortniansky's "Vesper Hymn," although Jackson does not refer to this in his discussion of the tune.[5] "Murillo's Lesson" (OSH 358) seems to have been taken from a piece for fife in an *Instructor in Martial Music* published in Exeter, New Hampshire, in 1820.[6] "Long Time Ago" (SH 313) is an old-time popular song, by George Pope Morris and Charles Edward Horn, published in 1837.[7] There are in addition two German tunes: "Krambambuli," a drinking song, becomes a temperance plea in "O Come Come Away" (OSH 334, SH 144), while "Soft Music" (OSH 323) is the familiar "Du, du liegst mir im Herzen." "Welch" (SH 109) is "All Through the Night." The title is obviously a misspelling of "Welsh," and, of course, it may be argued that Wales is at least a part of Britain.

But folk song backgrounds will be taken up in the next chapter, so let us now return to the question of scales used.

The melodies written in a seven-tone scale are all major or minor; there are no modal melodies, strictly speaking. It is true that most of the minor tunes are in the Aeolian form of minor, but this may be due to the deficiencies of most shape-note printing. Indeed, "Lena" (OSH 210) is printed with the raised seventh, while this is omitted in *The Supplement to the Kentucky Harmony.* There are twenty-one major melodies and sixteen minor. Of the minor melodies, Jackson was unable to find satisfactory folk song backgrounds for seven; this is true also for twelve of the major tunes.

It is comparatively easy to classify a melody as "pentatonic," "basically pentatonic," or "hexatonic." "Pentatonic" simply means that the melody is constructed with five tones; using seven-syllable solmization these tones would be do, re, mi, sol, and la. A melody basically pentatonic is one in which the missing tones may appear once or twice as unessential elements; in the terms of traditional harmony these are usually passing tones. "Hexatonic" melodies are those which definitely use six

5. George Pullen Jackson, *Another Sheaf of White Spirituals,* no. 236.
6. *Ibid.,* no. 134.
7. "Long Time Ago" is one of five *Old American Songs* arranged by Aaron Copland and recorded by William Warfield on Columbia ML 2206. The information about the song comes from the notes on the record jacket by Morris Hastings.

tones, those of the pentatonic scale plus either "fa" or "ti." It is less easy to discover the mode of certain of these melodies, and it is even harder to discuss the question of mode because of the varying terminologies in use by folklorists.

The present system of nomenclature has been arrived at after a long period of time, principally through a study of Joseph Yasser's *A Theory of Evolving Tonality*. More recently these theories have been crystallized by a study of the two volumes of *The Traditional Tunes of the Child Ballads* by Bertrand Bronson.

Four modes are in common use in the folk hymns: Ionian (or major), Aeolian (natural minor), Mixolydian, and Dorian, in order of frequency. It is significant that these are also the most common modes used in English secular folk song.[8] These, untransposed, are shown in Ex. 6.

Ex. 6. Pentatonic scales

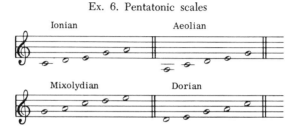

Ex. 7. Septatonic scales

Instead of the elaborate systems of designating the pentatonic scales used by Sharp and by Bronson, the author has preferred to think of these five-tone scales as the original forms of the Ionian, Aeolian, Mixolydian, and Dorian modes. The seven-tone versions simply fill in the gaps (Ex. 7).

The hexatonic scales present a little more difficulty. The scale C-D-E-

8. Cecil Sharp, *English Folk-Song: Some Conclusions* (London, 1907), pp. 54, 55.

F-G-A-C could theoretically be either Ionian, assuming B natural as the missing tone, or Mixolydian if this tone were B flat. Similarly the scale C-D-E-G-A-B-C could be Ionian if the missing note were F, or Lydian if it were F sharp. The possibilities for the four modes would therefore be as shown in Ex. 8.

Ex. 8. Hexatonic scales

Bronson simply gives a dual analysis for melodies written in these scales. Thus a melody written in the scale of I-A above would be classi- fied as I/M (Ionian or Mixolydian); one in the scale of I-B would be I/L; one in the scale of II-A would be Ae/Ph, and so on. There are two objections to this type of analysis. The first is simple enough: the Lydian and Phrygian modes are almost nonexistent in Anglo-American folk song. The second objection is more nebulous.

Today most musicians, particularly the theorists, are trained to analyze by ear as well as by eye. Thus many musicians familiar with modal music must have thought, like the author, while reading through a melody such as Bronson, I, p. 19, no. 23, "Why that is Aeolian, not Dorian." The ear recognizes the essential character of the mode despite the missing note of the scale.

In the preface to her edition of Sharp's *English Folk Songs from the Southern Appalachians*, Miss Karpeles says that she has determined the mode in some puzzling examples by locating the weak tones of the melody.[9] In attempting to rationalize the feeling for a certain mode in many of those hexatonic melodies marked by Bronson as having dual modality, the author has conversely looked for the strong notes in the melodic line, i.e., the melodic skips and accented notes. If we accept the Yasser theory that a hexatonic scale is a pentatonic scale in the process of being filled in, then those strong notes will be those of the pentatonic scale.

It must be admitted that by no means all of the hexatonic melodies in the two Bronson volumes may be assigned a definite mode by means of the methods outlined above. After all, Gregorian chant sometimes presents what Apel calls "modal ambiguity."[10] Gregorian chant is also a body of melody that, in its early days at least, was handed down by oral tradition. Miss Karpeles also noted that certain secular folk melodies were ambiguous.[11] Any melody is apt to suffer when it is passed along to other singers; some people have better tonal memory than others. At any rate, a large proportion of the Bronson melodies may be given a definite mode by means of the above methods.[12]

Still, using the Jackson list, sixty of the tunes are found to be in a hexatonic scale with "ti" as the extra tone. Of these, thirty-eight, not counting duplications, are in the Aeolian minor, eighteen are in major (Ionian), and four are in Dorian. Of hexatonic tunes with "fa," thirty-one are in major and six are in Mixolydian, while only one is in Aeolian.

Pentatonic tunes and those that are basically pentatonic have been

9. Page xix. See also the Introduction to the 1917 edition.
10. *Gregorian Chant,* pp. 166 ff.
11. Sharp-Karpeles, vol. I, no. 20, B; no. 41, A; etc.
12. Those interested in this analysis of the Bronson melodies should see the unpublished *magna cum laude* thesis by James Stivers in the Library of the Jordan College of Music of Butler University, Indianapolis, Ind.

grouped together. Lest there be any question about the term "basically pentatonic," an example (Ex. 9) is herewith given.

In this group, ninety-four are major (Ionian), thirty-one are Aeolian, twelve are Mixolydian, and seven are Dorian. As to the latter mode,

Ex. 9. Morning Trumpet, NH 99. The scale used is essentially an Aeolian pentatonic on F.

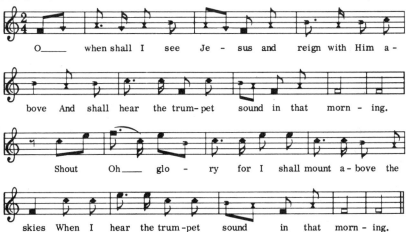

it must be mentioned that all Dorian tunes are written as Aeolians except for two tunes in *The Original Sacred Harp*, "Villulia" (OSH 56) and "Jordan's Shore" (OSH 50). Though the signature for each indicates the Aeolian, the sixth degree is raised in both tunes; this, of course, is extremely rare in shape-note books. And it is quite true, as Dr. Jackson noted, that Dorian tunes are sung as Dorian whether the raised sixth is printed or not.[13] Unfortunately, certain groups also raise the sixth in tunes that are unmistakably Aeolian. The author has heard East Tennessee groups turn "New Topia" from Aeolian into Dorian many, many times.

The rhythmic and metric factors are not nearly so clear-cut. Here are some signs that may point to a folk origin of a tune:

a. If a tune begins on an upbeat, particularly in quadruple simple or duple compound meters, this note is apt to be of longer duration (Ex. 10). This may possibly be an inheritance from Scottish and English psalmody.

13. George Pullen Jackson, *Spiritual Folk-Songs of Early America*. See the discussion of "Wondrous Love," p. 115.

b. The following rhythmic patterns are typical:

(1) 3/2 ♩♩ ♩♩ . This is frequently misbarred as 2/2.[14] Correct barring is arrived at through scansion of the text, thus:

Thŏu Mán ŏf gríef rĕ-mém-bĕr mé
Thŏu név-er cánst Thy-sélf fŏr-gét.

In "Kedron" (SH 3) this text is set as shown in Ex. 11. It should obviously be rebarred so that the word "man" and the first syllable of "never" come on strong beats (Ex. 12).

Ex. 10. Webster, OSH 31

Come   we who love the   Lord   And   let our   joys   be   Known

Join   in   a   song   with sweet ac - cord   And   thus   sur - round the throne.

Ex. 11

Thou Man of   grief   re-mem-ber me Thou nev- er canst Thy - self for - get

Ex. 12

Thou   Man   of grief re-mem-ber me Thou   nev- er canst Thy - self for -get

Any of these beats may be divided, but the pattern is always recognizable by the strong secondary accent on the second beat, unlike the normal triple simple metric scheme. Only eight tunes have this pattern all the way through, but it is a feature of many of the mixed-meter melodies.
(2) 3/4 ♩♪♪ mixed with ♩ ♩ . This is also carried over into 6/4 (or 6/8): ♩♫♩♩ . It is never misbarred, and the pattern occurs in twenty tunes.
(3) 4/4 or 2/2: ♩♫♩♫ . This pattern occurs in twenty-four tunes.

14. Jackson, *White Spirituals*, p. 133.

(4) 4/4 or 2/2: 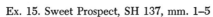 . Unlike the preceding patterns, which may or may not have an upbeat, this one always begins with a half note on the second half of the measure. It is one of the measure forms referred to in (a) above. It occurs ten times.

(5) 6/4: . This is the same type of pattern in duple compound meter. It occurs eight times.

(6) 6/8 (or 6/4): mixed with . This occurs twenty times.

c. Mixed meters. Sixty-four tunes have mixed meters, and all except one of these is also misbarred. The exception is "Pastoral Elegy" (SH 147), where measures of duple compound (6/8) alternate with measures of triple simple (3/4). This is obviously a misprint.[15] Nevertheless, as printed in *The Southern Harmony*, the tune appears as shown in Ex. 13. Most misbarrings involve 3/2 as in pattern (1) and a simple 2/2 with four quarter notes to the measure (Ex. 14). Less frequent is the same sort of thing in duple and triple compound, as in "Sweet Prospect" (Ex. 15).

Ex. 13. Pastoral Elegy

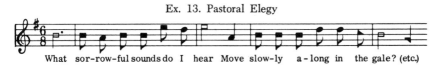

What sor-row-ful sounds do I hear Move slow-ly a-long in the gale? (etc.)

Ex. 14. Liverpool, SH 1, mm. 1–5

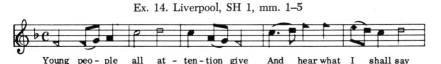

Young peo-ple all at-ten-tion give And hear what I shall say

Rebarred

Young peo-ple all at-ten-tion give And hear what I shall say

Ex. 15. Sweet Prospect, SH 137, mm. 1–5

On Jor-dan's storm-y banks I stand And cast a wish-ful eye

15. In *The Sacred Melodeon* (1849) and elsewhere the tune has two equal dotted notes in alternate measures.

"Sweet Prospect" is a Dorian tune, and to be completely correct, tonally as well as rhythmically, it should look like Ex. 16.

There are three factors in the formal-constructional aspect of a folk hymn, though only two of these are of unique importance and will be dealt with in this chapter. (The actual patterns of phrase repetition

Ex. 16. Sweet Prospect, mm. 1-5, rebarred. Key signature shows Dorian Mode.

  On   Jor - dan's storm-y banks I stand And cast a wish - ful eye

will be treated in a later chapter.) First, the *shape* of the tune is important. Willi Apel recognized the validity of shape as a stylistic factor when he said, "The basic design of a Gregorian melody is that of an arch whose apex is reached and left in wavy lines formed mostly by ascending and descending seconds, but also including larger intervals, particularly thirds."[16] Similarly, the basic design of a folk hymn is apt to be a series of arches: a small, a large, and another small. This basic shape changes very little from mode to mode. In four-phrase tunes the large arch is formed by phrases two and three; in six-phrase tunes it is formed by phrases three and four. Note Ex. 17 and 18.

In all, 168 tunes show this arch form; in addition 27 more show it in modified form, i.e., only one of the middle phrases rises abruptly. Generally speaking, tunes not having this distinctive profile belong to three classes: fuguing pieces (Jackson includes a few as having folk song backgrounds), tunes with long refrains, and tunes having an uneven number of phrases.

The second point to be made concerns typical melodic figures. First of all let us look at the cadence figures, those last few notes before the end of a tune. Though this will be discussed much more fully under the subject of centonization, we may sum up the matter here by saying that the final in each mode is typically approached from above, stepwise along the scale involved. In the pentatonic scale of each mode, and even in the hexatonic-with-ti of the Dorian, these hypothetical cadence figures would be those given in Ex. 19.

Only in the Ionian and Aeolian modes is the final ever approached from below, although in all modes an occasional ornament may be added after the true cadence formula has been completed. Cadence formulae

16. *Gregorian Chant*, p. 249.

in which the final is approached from below occur in 20 to 25 per cent of Ionian tunes, but these will be taken up later.

Ex. 17. Ester, OSH 37, four phrases

Young la-dies all at - ten-tion give You that in wick - ed pleas-ures

live One of your sex the oth-er day Was called by death's cold hand a - way.

Ex. 18. The Enquirer, OSH 74, rebarred. Dorian, but in Aeolian notation.

I'm not a-shamed to own my Lord Or to de - fend His cause
Main-tain the hon - or of His Word The glo - ry of His Cross

Je - sus my God I know His name His name is all my trust

Nor will He put my soul to shame Nor let my hope be lost.

Ex. 19

Ionian (major)   Aeolian   Mixolydian   Dorian

Ex. 20. New Britain, OSH 45

A - maz -ing grace how sweet the sound That saved a wretch like

me I__ once was lost but now I'm found Was blind but now I see.

The next most significant bit of figure construction occurs in the middle of the tune. But before going into this it is necessary to mention two patterns of phrase repetition that really belong in a later chapter. The first is the four-phrase form ABBA or ABB'A. The second is the six-phrase form AB CD AB, a perfectly normal three-part song form.

Ex. 21. Davis, SH 15

O Thou in whose pres - ence my soul takes de - light

On whom in af - flic - tion I call My com - fort by day and my

song in the night My hope my sal - va - tion my all.

Ex. 22. Idumea, NH 44

Come ye that __ love the __ Lord And let your joys be known

Join in a __ song with sweet ac - cord While ye sur - round His throne.

Ex. 23. Fiducia, SH 92, rebarred

Fath - er I long I faint to see The place of Thine a - bode
I'd leave these earth - ly courts and flee Up to Thy courts my God

Here I be - hold Thy dis - tant face And 'tis a pleas - ing

sight But to a - bide in Thine em - brace Is in - fin - ite de - light.

Now the form ABBA is not very common outside of folk music; in fact, particularly if one of the other factors mentioned in this chapter is present, the form is a good indication of folk origin. However, in tunes not actually having the ABBA form, some reference to it is frequently made in that a figure from phrase two is characteristically repeated in phrase three. See Ex. 20–22. This peculiarity of figure construction may also be seen in "Sing to Me of Heaven" at the beginning of this chapter.

Ex. 24. The Saints Bound for Heaven, OSH 35

In six-phrase tunes the normal three-part form as illustrated in Ex. 16 may also be varied somewhat in that phrase five, although ending like phrase one, begins with a new figure. Frequently this figure is one that occurs in one of the middle phrases (Ex. 23 and 24).

In conclusion, let us try a bit of stylistic analysis on "Abbeville," a tune not listed in the Jackson books. It occurs in *The Original Sacred Harp*, both revisions, page 33, as shown in Ex. 25. First of all, it is in the modified pentatonic scale of G major, with two passing tones "ti" at the end of phrases one and four. Second, it is in one of the typical rhythmic patterns: triple simple meter with a half and two eighths in eight of the thirteen measures. Third, it has the usual arch form. Fourth, while it cannot be said to be a true ABBA form, it has a distinctive figure from the second phrase carried over into the third.

"Abbeville" is almost certainly a folk hymn. If not, it is an extraordinarily good imitation.

IV

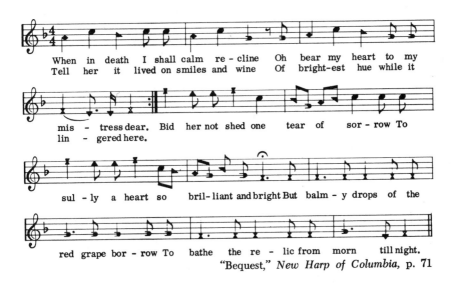

When in death I shall calm re-cline Oh bear my heart to my
Tell her it lived on smiles and wine Of bright-est hue while it

mis - tress dear. Bid her not shed one tear of sor - row To
lin - gered here.

sul - ly a heart so bril-liant and bright But balm - y drops of the

red grape bor - row To bathe the re - lic from morn till night.

"Bequest," *New Harp of Columbia,* p. 71

T HE WORDS, believe it or not, are by Thomas Moore. One of the minor
delights of an Old Harp singing in East Tennessee is to hear "Bequest" shouted out by fifty or more pillars of the various denominations,
many of whom are members of the local WCTU. It is extremely popular.

The tune is an oral-tradition form of the well-known "Vesper Hymn"
by Bortniansky.[1] In other words, "Bequest" is a contrafactum, a term
which Apel defines as "a vocal composition in which the original text is
replaced by a new one, particularly a secular text by a sacred one and
vice versa."[2]

Chapter III made the point that many tunes based on a seven-tone
scale are contrafacti of songs that are, or were, widely known. In addition
to the tunes mentioned in the preceding chapter other well-known tunes
adapted to sacred words are the following:

1. Another oral-tradition version of this tune, "Weeping Saviour," has been noted
in Chapter III.
2. *Harvard Dictionary,* p. 183.

1. Bruce's Address, SH 132, NH 109, is "Scots what hae wi' Wallace Bled," a tune more popular in the past than in our own generation.[3] It is discussed by Dr. Jackson in SF 112 under the title "Friends of Freedom."
2. Celebration, NH 118, is "O Where and O Where has my Highland Laddie Gone." It is not included in the Jackson books.
3. Home, NH 54, and Sweet Home, SH 251, are "Home Sweet Home." The tune appears frequently under some such title, although in *The Christian Minstrel*, p. 291, it is disguised somewhat as "Saint's Home."[4]
4. Joyful, NH 141, is the English carol "Joys Seven."[5] Jackson includes it in SF 227.
5. Long Ago, NH 183, and When I am Gone, SH 305, are "Long Long Ago." It is not mentioned by Jackson.
6. Plenary, SH 262, OSH 162, and Hamburg, NH 111, are "Auld Lang Syne."

When we come to sacred versions of the less well-known folk tunes, we are on more debatable grounds. In the first place, the true folk song, passed along by oral tradition, is constantly changing, and who is to say what it sounded like 100 or 150 years ago? Many folk tunes, it is true, have preserved their identity remarkably. Examples 26 and 27 are unmistakably the same, or at least descended from the same melodic ancestor, despite the change of mode and the generally more sophisticated nature of the English tune.

Another tune is one of the oldest in folk hymnody in America. It appears in Ingalls' *Christian Harmony* as "Shouting Hymn" (Ex. 28).

The American versions of the tune—and there are many—are all in minor. Unfortunately, *English Folk Songs for Schools* is not dated, but

Ex. 26. Clamanda, OSH 42, rebarred (music only)

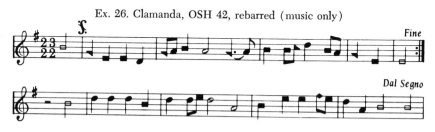

3. Butterworth-Brown, p. 335.
4. This tune appears frequently in the manuals of the nineteenth century under similar titles.
5. Percy Dearmer, R. Vaughan Williams, and Martin Shaw, *The Oxford Book of Carols*, no. 70.

since the Reverend Mr. Baring-Gould, the older of the two collaborators, was not born until 1834, it is obvious that this version is later than that of the "Shouting Hymn" of 1805. The tune is undoubtedly English, how-

Ex. 27. Just as the Tide was Flowing, *English Folk Songs for Schools*[6]

Ex. 28. Rebarred, transposed from A minor

ever, and was probably sung in both sacred and secular versions long before 1805.[7]

A similar case may be made for the tune "Davis," SH 15. Though the *Methodist Hymnal* of 1886 attributes the tune to Freeman Lewis, the writer has been unable to find it in either *The Beauties of Harmony* of 1814 or in *Songs of Zion* of 1824. The first appearance of "Davis" may have been in Part Second of Wyeth's *Repository of Sacred Music* (p. 81) of 1813. From that time on it appears frequently in the shape-note books under varying titles. Compare Ex. 29 and 30.

6. Sabine Baring-Gould and Cecil Sharp, *English Folk-Songs for Schools*, p. 52.
7. Jackson, *Spiritual Folk-Songs*, no. 93.

Again, the two tunes undoubtedly have a common ancestor. That the tune was known in America long before its appearance in the *Repository* is quite probable, since its first phrase is centonized in at least two eighteenth-century tunes (Ex. 31 and 32).

Ex. 29. Davis, SH 15 (music only)

Ex. 30. Fair Rosie Ann, *Last Leaves of Traditional Ballads and Ballad Airs,*[8] transposed from D major

Ex. 31. Warsaw, *Harmonia Americana*[9]

Ex. 32. Redemption, *Social Harmony*[10]

Much more puzzling is the ancestry of the tune "Pisgah," SH 80, OSH 58. Though Jackson indicates a folk song background for this, which the author has been unable to check, he himself notes that *The Methodist Hymn Book of England* names the tune "Covenanters" and calls it an American melody.[11] *The Story of the Hymns and Tunes* says it is " . . .

8. Gavin Greig and Alexander Keith, *Last Leaves of Traditional Ballads and Ballad Airs.*
9. Samuel Holyoke, *Harmonia Americana.*
10. Asahel Benham, *Social Harmony.*
11. *Spiritual Folk-Songs,* no. 123.

an old revival piece by J. C. Lowry (1820), once heard in many camp-meetings. . . ."[12] The OSH gives exactly the same author and date. Example 33 gives the tune as it appears in *The Original Sacred Harp*, both revisions. The tune is then repeated with a few unessential flourishes.

Millar Patrick speaks of an attempt in the present century to revive older Scottish psalmody in a volume called *Old Scottish Psalm Tunes*. In this volume there were ". . . many tunes no older than the last century. . . . A fair number were American. . . . In the last class was one arch-

Ex. 33. Pisgah, OSH 58

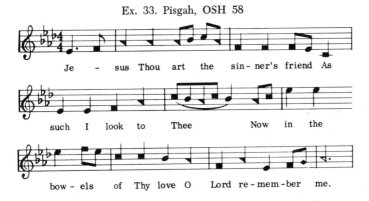

Ex. 34. Covenanters, words "The Race that Long in Darkness Pined," *The Hymnbook*, no. 153

deceiver named 'Covenanters' which imposed itself upon the credulous as a genuine survivor from Covenanting times."[13] "Covenanters" would seem to be our old friend "Pisgah," and under the first name it appears in the new *Hymnbook* (1955) of the Presbyterian Churches (Ex. 34).

Perhaps someone else can determine the amount and direction of lend-lease involved here.

While "Pisgah" is certainly open to doubt as being descended from British folk song, in general Jackson's sources are quite correct. The author spent a summer checking these in the British Museum and at

12. Butterworth-Brown, p. 118.
13. *Four Centuries of Scottish Psalmody*, p. 188.

Cecil Sharp House and turned up only a few in which the relationship seemed tenuous. Frequently these were tunes in which the "finding of secular analogies was limited . . . to melodic parts instead of whole tunes" as noted in Chapter III. Some are discussed in Chapter VI.

Another tune whose ancestry is doubtful, however, is "Garden Hymn," SH 90. Although Jackson discusses the tune in DE 158, its ancestry is given in "Ceylon," SF 132, a tune closely related to "Garden Hymn." Actually, the tune in some form or another has appeared in many books, beginning with Ingalls' *Christian Harmony*, where it is called "Love Divine." Other versions, among many, occur in *The Supplement to the Kentucky Harmony* ("Baltimore"), *The Timbrel of Zion* ("Bexley"), and *The Sacred Melodeon* ("Ceylon"). OSH 64 has a somewhat more elaborate version (but with the same words as "Garden Hymn") called "Nashville." Jackson relates this group of tunes, through "Ceylon," to "The Ribbonman's March," no. 993 in Petrie's *Complete Collection of Irish Music*, a relationship not apparent to the eyes or ears of this writer.

On the other hand, the author located a few British backgrounds that Jackson missed. "Dublin," "Tennessee," and "Elysian" are discussed elsewhere in this book. A puzzling omission in the Jackson canon is "Judgment," SH 47, for the tune is to be found in Chappell, *Popular Music of the Olden Times*, pp. 748–49. The author says of it, " . . . Primitive Methodists or Ranters . . . collect airs sung at pot and public houses and write their hymns to them." The tune is also included in Annabel Morris Buchanan's *Folk Hymns of America*, as no. 2, and is called "Rise My Soul." With Chappell, she notes that the tune is a "Ranter's Hymn."

Now the curious thing about all this is that "Judgment" has always reminded this author of the standard hymn tune "Amsterdam." "Amsterdam" is one of the earliest Methodist hymns, for it appeared in their first published hymnal, *A Collection of Tunes as they are Commonly Sung at the Foundery*, published in 1742. Furthermore, "Amsterdam" also begins with the words "Rise my Soul," as indeed does "Judgment." "Amsterdam" is usually attributed to Dr. James Nares, organist at York Cathedral in 1734 and at the Chapel Royal in 1756. Did "Amsterdam" derive from "The Ranter's Hymn," or is the latter a folk version of the more dignified hymn tune?

There can be no question that "Captain Kidd," SH 50, is an excellent example of a contrafactum (Ex. 35). Its very title admits its secular origin. The tune has been used with sacred words at least ever since Ingall's time, for it appears in *The Christian Harmony* as "Honor to the Hills" with the same text that is used in *The Southern Harmony* thirty years later.[14] The tune is also known as "Green Meadow" from the reference in the penultimate line.[15] The secular version of the song is given in Ex. 36.

Ex. 35. Captain Kidd, SH 50

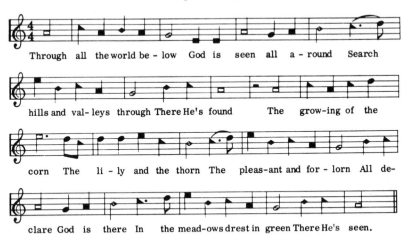

Through all the world be-low God is seen all a-round Search hills and val-leys through There He's found The grow-ing of the corn The li-ly and the thorn The pleas-ant and for-lorn All de-clare God is there In the mead-ows drest in green There He's seen.

Ex. 36. Captain Kidd, *Our Familiar Songs and Who Made Them*[16]

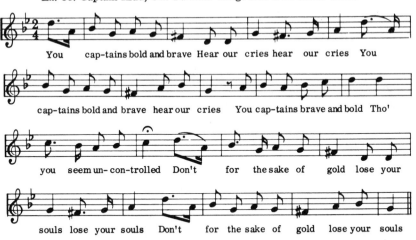

You cap-tains bold and brave Hear our cries hear our cries You cap-tains bold and brave hear our cries You cap-tains brave and bold Tho' you seem un-con-trolled Don't for the sake of gold lose your souls lose your souls Don't for the sake of gold lose your souls

14. Jeremiah Ingalls, *Christian Harmony or Songster's Companion.*
15. It is so known in *The Supplement to the Kentucky Harmony, The Missouri Harmony,* and *The Knoxville Harmony.*
16. Helen Kendrick Johnson, *Our Familiar Songs and Who Made Them,* p. 171. The author says, "I can learn nothing of the history of the ballad, but it is evidently of English origin."

The tunes of many folk hymns are like or similar to tunes used for secular songs and ballads of American origin, particularly those of the southeastern part of the country. In the case of "Service of the Lord," OSH 80, Jackson makes an important suggestion:[17] "The tune 'Service of the Lord' . . . seems to have been borrowed by those who sang 'Little Musgrave and Lady Barnard' as it is found in Sharp, i, 162. Indications

Ex. 37. Transposed when necessary (words omitted)

that the direction of borrowing was as suggested may be found in the misfit of words to tune in the secular song. . . ." And why not? The writer would like to suggest that, in the case where no background of English folk song has been found but where an American folk song has been found to be like a folk hymn, the secular has been borrowed from the sacred in some instances. Let us examine two of them.

The folk hymn "To Die no More," OSH 111, is exactly like a secular folk song called "The Three Crows" in *Traditional Ballads of Virginia*,

17. *Spiritual Folk-Songs*, no. 215.

recorded in Norfolk County in 1919.[18] But the simple two-phrase tune is also well known as a hymn called "Going Home"; it is to be found in the *Methodist Hymnal* for 1886,[19] and in *Hymns and Songs of Praise,* an interdenominational standard hymnal printed in 1874.[20] It also may be found in books of gospel songs up into the twentieth century and in many singing school manuals of northern origin. It is almost invariably attributed to William Miller. The three tunes are given for comparison in Ex. 37.

Ex. 38. Transposed when necessary (words omitted)

1. Meditation

2. Bourbon

3. Samuel Young

Though the direction of borrowing may be inconclusive in the above example, the next instance is rather more than probable. This is "Meditation," SH 4, which is a starker version of the older "Bourbon," attributed to Freeman Lewis and appearing in his *Beauties of Harmony* of 1814. The name "Bourbon" would seem to commemorate that greatest of all camp meetings held at Cane Ridge, Bourbon County, Kentucky,

18. Arthur Kyle Davis, *Traditional Ballads of Virginia.*
19. Page 404.
20. Edited by Hitchcock, Eddy, and Schaff, p. 281. The tune is here attributed to William Miller.

at the turn of the nineteenth century.[21] Be that as it may, "Bourbon" certainly dates from no later than 1814. It appears to be true "unwritten music" in that it has a number of variants in both northern and southern manuals.[22] It also has a secular version, the American ballad "Samuel Young," recorded in Burnsville, North Carolina, in 1918.[23] It is the second verse of this ballad that gives the clue as to its date:

He wed in London, Kentucky state
It was in eighteen forty-eight.
The call was in for men to go
To these lowlands of Mexico.

In other words, the ballad obviously comes a long time after the hymn. A comparison of the three tunes will show the similarity (Ex. 38).

All this is, of course, a matter of conjecture and needs much more investigation. It is a field that should offer considerable interest to the true folklorist.

But in the end, a good tune is a good tune, no matter whether the words are sacred or worldly. And I strongly suspect that this is the way the folk singers have felt about the matter.

21. Sweet, *Religion in the Development of American Culture*, p. 149.
22. "Peace" in *The Revivalist*; "Dismission" in Caldwell's *Union Harmony*; "Lord's Supper" in Walker's *Christian Harmony*.
23. Sharp-Karpeles, II, 271.

V

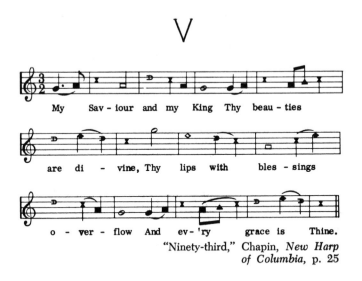

My Sav - iour and my King Thy beau - ties
are di - vine, Thy lips with bles - sings
o - ver - flow And ev - 'ry grace is Thine.

"Ninety-third," Chapin, *New Harp of Columbia*, p. 25

T HE NAME "Chapin" turns up again and again in the singing school manuals and even in the standard hymnals of the nineteenth century. Sometimes the name is preceded by the initial *L* or *A*; sometimes the Christian name Amzi is given. *The Original Sacred Harp*, confusing an *a* and an *o*, even attributes a tune called "Vernon" to F. F. Chapin.[1] The Polish composer would doubtless be very much surprised.

Since the name "Chapin" is attached with reasonable frequency to no less than eight of the most popular folk hymns, it would seem that we have here a folk composer of considerable ability. Actually, as Charles Hamm has shown, there were no less than seven singing masters, in two generations, with this surname.[2] The most likely composer for the seven tunes would be either Lucius (1760-1842) or Amzi (1768-1835), and Hamm makes out a strong case for Lucius, based on tunes named for places with which he was associated.

Which of the Chapins was actually the composer of any given tune is immaterial to this study. What is important is that most of the tunes

1. Page 95.
2. "The Chapins."

attributed to "Chapin" seem to have been freely composed, with no re-
course to specific folk songs and little to centonization. "Ninety-third," a
very early tune, was one of these. Others are the following:

1. Golden Hill, NH 81. This is attributed to "Aaron Chapin" in some
   standard hymnals.[3] Aaron was a brother of Lucius and Amzi
   Chapin and lived between 1753 and 1828. Charles Hamm, however, does not believe him to have composed any of the tunes
   attributed to "Chapin" in the Old Harp books.[4] Jackson in DE 86
   and AnS 229 says it is a member of the Lord Lovel family and
   gives a large variety of English folk songs of the same general
   trend. One of these, "The Mermaid," Sharp 291, does have a
   second phrase that is the same. Butterworth-Brown claim that the
   tune was suggested by the song of the wood thrush, and that "old
   time folk" used to call it "Sing my Fairweather Bird."[5]
2. Olney, SH 64, OSH 135. Jackson gives no folk song background
   in DE 70.
3. Primrose, SH 3, OSH 47. Jackson gives no folk song background
   in DE 165.
4. Rockbridge, SH 288. Jackson, in AnS 204, gives Petrie 800 and
   1494 as references. There may be some slight resemblance between the first phrases of both of these and the first phrase of
   "Rockbridge," but it is very slight indeed.
5. Rockingham, SH 300. Jackson lists no generating folk song in DE
   150.
6. Tribulation, SH 119, OSH 29. Of the Jackson references given
   in SF 69, only one appears to be relevant: "The Bonnie Mermaid"
   in Motherwell, Supplement, no. 30.[6]
7. Vernon, SH 34, OSH 95. DE 19 gives no folk song background.

The tune "Albion," SH 23, OSH 52, NH 12, is another tune that seems
to have been freely composed. Jackson was unable to supply a folk song
background for it, remarking simply that "It sounds like one of the old
psalm tunes."[7] In all three of the books used in this study it is attributed
to "Boyd"; elsewhere it is sometimes attributed to "Robert Boyd."
"Albion" seems to have appeared first in *The Kentucky Harmony* of
Ananias Davisson, c. 1815. It is reasonable to suppose that its composer
was the "Captain R. Boyd" mentioned in the Knoxville "Register" of May

3. *Hymns and Songs of Praise,* no. 190.
4. There are several other tunes attributed to "Chapin." See Hamm, "The Chapins," and Lowens, "John Wyeth's *Repository.*"
5. Page 108.
6. William Motherwell, *Minstrelsy, Ancient and Modern* (Glasgow, 1827).
7. *Spiritual Folk-Songs,* no. 78.

26, 1818, as being a friend and colleague of Davisson. "Boyd" is also given as the composer of "Salvation," SH 84, NH 24, but there can be no doubt that this very popular tune belongs to the "unwritten music" class.[8] Boyd may have harmonized the tune, and it is significant that "Salvation" too seems to have appeared first in *The Kentucky Harmony*.

The tune "Babylonian Captivity" is not listed in the Jackson books, but it has many of the hallmarks we have been associating with the folk hymns: it is in a gapped scale (hexatonic with ti—the two fas are non-harmonic), it has the typical arch shape, and it is in a mixed 2/2–3/2 meter (Ex. 39). The words, a paraphrase of Psalm 137, are by the Hon. Joel Barlow and were written about 1799.[9] Barlow, born in Redding, Connecticut, had served as a chaplain in the Continental Army and later became ambassador to France. He died near Cracow, Poland, in 1812.

Ex. 39. Babylonian Captivity, SH 164

A - long the banks where Ba - bel's cur - rent flows Our cap - tive bands in deep de - spond-ence stray'd While Zi - on's fall in sad re-mem-brance rose Her friends her chil-dren min-gled with the dead.

The very beautiful tune is always attributed to "Dare." This is probably the Rev. Elkanah Kelsey Dare, who lived between 1782 and 1826. Dare was a "Methodist clergyman, Freemason, and musician" who had also served as dean of boys at Delaware College and in all probability was the musical editor of Wyeth's *Repository of Sacred Music, Part Second*.[10] This northern mine of folk hymns, dated 1813, has been shown by Irving Lowens to have had a great effect on southern hymnody. "Babylonian Captivity" first appeared here.

Dare is also credited with "Kedron," another lovely tune. It is one of the few folk hymns to be included in the hymnal of the Episcopal Church.[11] "Kedron," SH 3, OSH 48, NH 45, was first published in *The*

8. *Ibid.*, no. 95.

9. Butterworth-Brown, pp. 242, 243.

10. Lowens, p. 122.

11. *The Hymnal of the Protestant Episcopal Church in the United States of America*, no. 81.

United States Harmony of Amos Pilsbury, Boston, 1799.[12] Dare would then have been seventeen years old. It is possible that he wrote the tune, but it is equally possible that it belongs to the "unwritten music" class. Jackson gives several references, among them "Samuel Young" which as we have seen is practically identical with "Meditation."[13] Dare is also credited with "Glasgow," which Jackson does not list but which Lowens considers a folk hymn.[14] Both "Kedron" and "Glasgow" are in the *Repository*.

Daniel Read is credited with the tune "Charlestown" under its northern title "Bartimeus" in many standard hymn books of the second half of the nineteenth century. Since Read lived between 1757 and 1836, the generally given date of 1804 for "Charlestown" would fit. However,

Ex. 40. Charlestown, OSH 52

"Mer - cy O Thou Son of Da - vid" Thus blind Bar - ti - me- us prayed

"Oth - ers by Thy word are sav-ed Now to me af - ford Thine aid."

this tune is unlike the other pieces credited to this composer, the fuguing piece "Sherburne" and the two hymn tunes "Windham" and "Winter" still found in the Old Harp books. "Charlestown" has the typical folk hymn arch with the revealing phrase structure ABB'A (Ex. 40). *The Original Sacred Harp* attributes the tune to Stephen Jenks, in whose *Delights of Harmony,* 1805, it may first have appeared.

The tune "Elysian," SH 100, OSH 139, presents a curious case. In the two books above it is set to a verse by Richard Kempenfelt, a British naval man of Swedish descent who lived between 1718 and 1782. It begins "Burst ye emerald gates" which has eight lines and the metric scheme 7. 6. 7. 6. 7. 7. 7. 7. The time signature is 6/4. The same tune, slightly altered to adjust to a double verse with seven syllables in each line and in duple simple time, is found under a variety of names in northern standard hymnals and singing school books and is always attributed to "Ives" or "E. Ives, jr." This can only be the Elan Ives, Jr., who brought out the *American Psalmody* with Deodatus Dutton in 1830.

12. Lowens, p. 119.
13. *Spiritual Folk-Songs,* no. 57.
14. Lowens, p. 188.

The suggestion of a folk song background comes not from Jackson (who does not comment on the tune in DE 78) but from the standard hymnal *Hymns and Songs of Praise* (1874) which says the tune is an Irish melody

Ex. 41 (words omitted)

Elysian, OSH 139

Ives, *Jasper and Gold* (1877), transposed

The Minstrel Boy, *The Golden Book of Favorite Songs*, transposed

Elysian

Ives (note that these two phrases are reversed)

The Minstrel Boy

Elysian

Ives

The Minstrel Boy

arranged by Elan Ives, Jr., in 1846.[15] The tune appears in *The American or Unionist Harmony* of 1831 under the title "Harrisonburg," and in the supplement to *The Kentucky Harmony* (1825) under the same name; in both cases it is in duple compound time. Is the editor of *Hymns and Songs of Praise* wrong in his date, his information as to the composer, or both? Or did both Ives and the folk hymn writers derive their different versions of the tune from an Irish folk song which Jackson failed to discover? Personally, the author thinks that this tune is an oral-tradition form of "The Minstrel Boy," a tune included in most books of home songs in the early part of this century and still widely known. Compare them in Ex. 41.

The tune known as "The Teacher's Farewell" in OSH 34 and attributed there to Elder E. Dumas is almost certainly by E. W. Dunbar, and is

Ex. 42. The Teacher's Farewell, OSH 34

known by his name in many standard hymnals of the nineteenth century.[16] *The Story of the Hymns and Tunes* calls "Dunbar" an old revival tune.[17] Jackson, in DE 84, finds a relationship between this tune and the English "Sprig of Thyme," and it is obvious that it has some of the characteristics of the folk hymn. Though the arch form is not as characteristic as usual, it does have like figures at the beginning of both second and third phrases (Ex. 42).

"The Bower of Prayer," SH 70, OSH 100, according to *The Story of the Hymns and Tunes,* is by Elder John Osborne, who composed both words and music.[18] Osborne was a New Hampshire preacher, and the date given for the composition of the work is 1815. *The Story of the Hymns and Tunes* adds that the tune may have been suggested by "a flute interlude by Haydn." *The Original Sacred Harp* gives the composer as

15. Look for it under the title "Beulah" here.
16. See, for instance, *Psalms and Hymns and Spiritual Songs: a Manual of Worship for The Church of Christ.*
17. Page 531.
18. Page 146.

"Osborn," through *The Southern Harmony* says "Richerson and White." Jackson, in DE 3, gives no folk song background.

There are many tunes always given with the same composer, but it is hard to find out anything about these men. For instance, both "America" (SH 27, OSH 36) and "Florida," a fuguing piece (SH 120, OSH 203) are attributed to a composer whose name is spelled variously as Whitmore, Wetmore, and Whetman.[19] *The Original Sacred Harp* gives the composer of "Florida" as Truman S. Wetmore and the date about 1808. It is at least six years older, for it appears in *The Easy Instructor* of 1802.[20] Jackson includes "America" in DE 187 but gives no folk song background. *The Original Sacred Harp* gives the date as 1832, but, as

Ex. 43. Kambia, SH 154

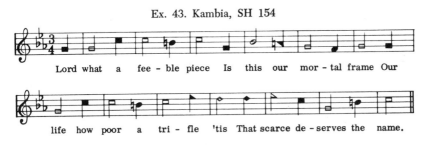

Lord what a fee - ble piece Is this our mor - tal frame Our

life how poor a tri - fle 'tis That scarce de - serves the name.

noted in Chapter II, it appears much earlier.[21] Since it is a typical fuguing piece and since it is found so early, it is included in the list of Early American compositions. "Knoxville" (SH 140) and "Washington" (SH 67) are both attributed to R. Monday, probably the singing master who held the first school in Knoxville in 1818. Jackson finds good folk song antecedents for both of these, and it seems probable that Monday merely arranged them.[22]

Before leaving the topic of composed tunes, there is one tune listed by Jackson that is almost certainly not a folk hymn and is not even composed in the idiom. This is the tune "Kambia" (Ex. 43). Jackson says that this hymn is to be found only in the Walker song books, and, because of the A natural in the second phrase, he postulates a Welsh origin.[23] Since the phrase in question ends on a cadence on G, it has always

19. In Walker's *Christian Harmony*, Benham's *Social Harmony*, and the Little-Smith *Easy Instructor*, respectively.

20. Page 14.

21. No. 2.

22. "Monday" is still a common name in Knoxville. The 1968 telephone directory lists forty-two people of this name, besides two real estate firms and a hotel.

23. *Down East Spirituals and Others*, no. 117.

seemed to the writer that, despite the F natural in the *Southern Harmony* version, this indicated a perfectly straightforward modulation to the dominant. This suspicion was confirmed when "Kambia" was found in Lowell Mason's *The Choir* of 1839. Now *The Choir* is definitely not a book of folk hymns (Mason was the apostle of "better music"), and "Kambia" is note for note as it appears in the *Southern Harmony* except that it does have the F sharp, thus confirming the modulation. Just to show that this is no isolated instance, "Kambia" appears twelve years later, complete with modulation, in *The Presbyterian Psalmodist* of 1851, a hymnal authorized by the General Assembly. The tune is also included in *The Christian Minstrel* of 1856.[24] In both cases it has the modulation to the dominant.

The music shows that "Kambia" is not written in a gapped scale, its rhythmic pattern never uses the half and two eighths that are so common in 3/4, the arch form is not present, it does not use mixed meter, and its form is ABAC. In fact, it has not a single characteristic of the typical folk hymn.

24. J. B. Aiken, *The Christian Minstrel*.

VI

CENTO (L.), CENTONE (It., a patchwork quilt). The term
and its derivatives "centonization" and "to centonize" are used
with reference to literary and musical works formed by selec-
tions from other works. . . . The term also applies to musical
melodies pieced together from pre-existent fragments. . . .

Harvard Dictionary of Music

AT A CERTAIN STAGE in the musical development of many civiliza-
tions it seems to have been the practice to fashion new melodies from
a large repertory of traditional melodic formulae. The nomos of ancient
Greece and the echos of Byzantium seem to have been formulae of this
type; the *Harvard Dictionary* article on "melody types" mentions also
the Syrian risqolo, the Javanese patet, the Hindu raga, the Arabian
maqam, the Russian popievki, and the Weisen or Tone of the Meister-
singer. "Wandering phrases," that is, conventional melodic formulae as
much as a phrase long, are by no means unknown in the German
chorales.[1]

Ex. 44. Possible pentatonic (and hexatonic) melodic cadences

The possibility of extensive centonization in the Old Harp books was
suggested by two things: first, by an occasional indirect reference to such
a practice in the Jackson books, as noted in Chapter III; second, by the

1. Note, for instance, the final phrases of "Ein feste Burg" (no. 250 in the
Breitkopf Edition of the Bach *371 Chorales*) and "Vom Himmel hoch" (no. 46).

similarity of final cadence melodies in gapped-scale melodies belonging to the same mode. Certain of these were postulated in Ex. 19 for the pentatonic scale, but they might conceivably also apply to the hexatonic scale. Let us review these and also take into account those cadences in which the final is approached from below (Ex. 44).

Ex. 45. Dorian cadences

Babe of Bethlehem, SH 78
The Enquirer, OSH 74
Jordan's Shore, OSH 50, SH 318, NH 177
Royal Band, OSH 360
Sweet Prospect, OSH 65, SH 137
Wondrous Love, OSH 159, SH 252, NH 143

Invocation, SH 193
Villulia, OSH 56

Repose, SH 151

Ex. 46. Mixolydian cadences (a)

Weeping Pilgrim, OSH 417

An Address for All, SH 99

Soda, NH 67
Louisiana, SH 62
Reflection, NH 13
Converted Thief, SH 9 (in 6/8)

Paradise, NH 68
Church's Desolation, OSH 89

Christian Warfare, SH 37

Dorian tunes have cadences of the first basic type, with perhaps a repeated note or an ornament at the end to take care of an additional syllable of the text (Ex. 45).

Mixolydian tunes also use only the first type of postulated cadence. In Ex. 46 all four notes are used.

Two other cadence forms omit the first note (Ex. 47).

There are few Aeolian cadences in the basic form (Ex. 48).

The most common Aeolian cadence of the first type has a lower neighbor tone between the final and its repetition (Ex. 49).

Ex. 47. Mixolydian cadences (b)

Anticipation, NH 75
Christian Contemplation, NH 48
Condescension, NH 312
Cusseta, OSH 73
Midnight Cry, SH 32
White, OSH 288

Bound for Canaan, OSH 82
Hallelujah, OSH 146 (in 6/8)

Ex. 48. Aeolian cadences (a)

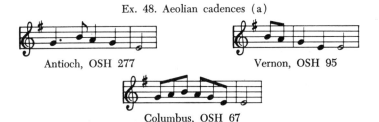

Antioch, OSH 277   Vernon, OSH 95

Columbus, OSH 67

Ex. 49. Aeolian cadences (b). There is some rhythmic variation in these.

Detroit, OSH 39
Distress, SH 22, OSH 32
Ecstasy, OSH 106
Good Physician, SH 49
Meditation, SH 4
Pilgrim, OSH 201
Save Mighty Lord, OSH 70
Wayfaring Stranger, OSH 457

Holy City, OSH 101
Messiah, OSH 131

Ex. 50. Aeolian cadences (c)

Consolation New, SH 58
Leander, SH 128
Morning Star, SH 115

The most common cadence using the "ti" of the typical Aeolian hexatonic scale is shown in Ex. 50.

In the Aeolian we see for the first time the final approached from below in the melodic line. All are variations of the second cadence postulated, which is basically mi-sol-la (Ex. 51).

There are, of course, a great many Ionian tunes, and a diversity of

Ex. 51. Aeolian cadences (d). Some of these have slight rhythmic variations.

Fight On, OSH 385
Hick's Farewell, SH 19
Solemn Thought, SH 29
Restoration, OSH 312

Fiducia, SH 92

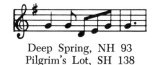

Sing to Me of Heaven, OSH 312

Ex. 52. Ionian cadences (a). The final is approached from above.

Ex. 53. Ionian cadences (b). The final is approached from below.

Christian Soldier, OSH 57, SH 45
Garden Hymn, SH 90
Judgment, SH 47
Pleasant Hill, NH 43, SH 66
Kingwood, SH 98, NH 83
Thorny Desert, SH 83
Dudley, SH 250
Farewell, NH 32
Greenfields, SH 71

Deep Spring, NH 93
Pilgrim's Lot, SH 138
Erie, NH 105

cadence formulae is to be expected. However, it is interesting to note that cadences in which the final is approached from above far outnumber those in which the final is approached from below. The former outnumber the latter about three to one. The most commonly found cadence melodies occur in duple compund meter (Ex. 52 and 53).

Another figure very common in major tunes occurs sometimes in the cadence and sometimes in other parts of the phrase. This figure occurs sometimes in tunes that are not, strictly speaking, folk hymns (Ex. 54).

Ex. 54. The examples given are in the tenor unless noted.

1. The Christian's Hope, OSH 206, phrase 1

We have our trou-bles here be - low

2. Christian Prospect, SH 323, phrases 1 and 3. Notice that this phrase and the one above are alike. Otherwise the two tunes are dissimilar.

We have our tri - als here be - low

3. Fairview, OSH 393, phrase 2, transposed

Of mor-tals here be - low

4. Infinite Day, OSH 446, phrase 1, transposed

There is a land of pure de - light

5. Jordan, OSH 439, phrase 8, transposed

And riv - ers of de - light

6. Manchester, OSH 392, phrases 1 and 8, transposed

There is a land of pure de - light

7. Morning Sun, OSH 436, phrase 1, transposed

Youth like the spring will soon be - gone

8. *Ibid.,* phrase 3

Your morn-ing sun may set at noon

9. *Ibid.,* phrase 4

And leave you ev - er in the dark

10. New Bethel, OSH 395, fugue, phrase 1

My gra - cious Mas-ter and my God

11. New Topia, NH 163, fugue, phrase 5 (soprano part)

Your joys on earth will soon be gone

12. Odem, OSH 340, phrase 2, transposed

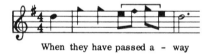

When they have passed a - way

13. Sacred Mount, OSH 456, phrase 1, transposed

Sing O ye ran-somed of the Lord

14. Warrenton, OSH 145, NH 66, phrase 1

Come thou fount of ev - 'ry bless-ing

The running-down of complete phrases is a much more fascinating job. Take, for instance, the tune "Albion," OSH 52, SH 23 (Ex. 55).

Ex. 55

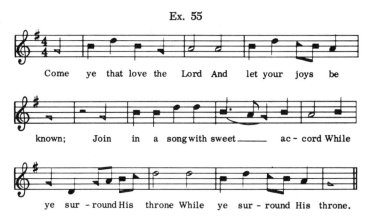

Come ye that love the Lord And let your joys be known; Join in a song with sweet———— ac - cord While ye sur - round His throne While ye sur - round His throne.

Ex. 56

1. Delight, fuguing piece, Stephen Jenks, *Musical Harmonist* (1800), phrases 1–2

2. Lynn, Daniel Belknap, *The Evangelical Harmony* (1800), phrases 1–2

3. Creation, Oliver Holden, *Worcester Harmony* (1803), phrases 1–2

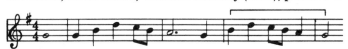

4. Montgomery, Jacob French, *The Psalmodist's Companion* (1793), last two phrases

5. Sheffield, Freeman Lewis, *The Beauties of Harmony* (1814), last two phrases

The cadence phrase, which is the same as the second except for the anacrusis, seems to have been one of the most commonly used phrases in New England hymnody. Note the following, all transposed, when necessary, into the key of G (Ex. 56). The phrase also occurs in slightly different rhythmic forms (Ex. 57).

Other tunes centonized to some extent from New England material

Ex. 57

1. Edgware, Samuel Holyoke, *Harmonia Americana* (1791), phrase 2

2. Aurora, Simeon Jocelyn and Amos Doolittle, *The Chorister's Companion* (1782–83), phrase 1

Ex. 58

1. Mary's Grief and Joy, OSH 451, phrases 1–2

Ma - ry at   her   Sav - iour's tomb   Hast - ed at the ear-ly   dawn

Cleansing Fountain, *Baptist Hymnal* (S) (1956), no. 92, transposed

There   is   a foun- tain   filled with blood Drawn from Im-man-u- els   veins

are "Babel's Streams" (SH 52, OSH 126), "Happy Matches" (OSH 96), and "Babylonian Captivity" (SH 164). See Appendix II for the last tune.

Several tunes have phrases taken from hymns familiar to most church-goers. Some of these are given for illustration though the centonized tunes appear neither in the Jackson list nor in Appendix II (Ex. 58).

One of the most widely used phrases, apparently, to originate in a folk hymn is the first phrase of "Tennessee." This, by the way, is one of the

2. Return Again, OSH 335, phrases 1–6

Sav- iour vis - it Thy plan -ta - tion Grant us Lord a gra-cious rain
All will come to de - so - la - tion Un - less Thou re -turn a -gain

Lord re - vive us, Lord re - vive us All our help must come from Thee

Nettleton, *Baptist Hymnal,* no. 313, transposed

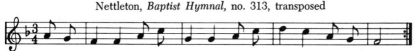

Come Thou fount of ev -'ry bless-ing Tune my heart to sing Thy grace
Streams of mer - cy nev - er ceas -ing Call for songs of loud- est praise

Teach me some me - lo-dious son - net Sung by flam-ing tongues a - bove

3. Elder, OSH 450, phrases 1–2

Gent - ly glides the stream of life Oft a - long the flow- ery vale

Toplady, *Baptist Hymnal,* no. 103, transposed. The rest of "Elder" is quite different from "Toplady."

Rock of ag - es cleft for me Let me hide my-self in Thee

few tunes in which the author was able to supplement the folk song background given by Jackson. Phrases 1, 2, 5, and 6 undoubtedly come from "May Colean" to be found in the musical appendix to Motherwell's *Minstrelsy Ancient and Modern.*[2] (Jackson's analysis applies to phrases 3 and 4 only.) "Tennessee" is an oral-tradition version of "Communion," a tune found in Lewis' *Beauties of Harmony* and other books of the early 1800s. Another version appears in Ingalls' *Christian Harmony* under

2. No. 24 in the appendix.

the title "Millennium." The first two phrases of "Tennessee" as it appears in SH 28 are shown in Ex. 59.

Example 60 would all seem to be versions of the same first phrase, no. 4 being from Appendix II.

Eight-phrase Mixolydian tunes have two types of middle section. There are five examples of the first type, which begins on "do" and ends on "re" or "sol" (Ex. 61).

Ex. 59

Af - flic - tions though they seem se - vere Are   oft in mer -cy sent

Ex. 60

1. Ragan, OSH 176, phrases 1–2

Fare - well vain world I'm go - ing home

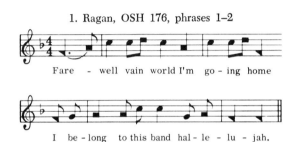

I be - long to this band hal - le - lu - jah.

2. Roll Jordan, OSH 274, phrases 1–2, transposed

He   comes He comes the judge se-vere   Roll   Jor -dan roll

3. Resurrected, OSH 153, phrases 1–2

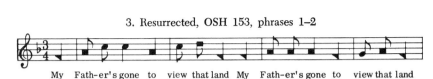

My Fath-er's gone to view that land My Fath-er's gone to   view that land

4. Mt. Zion, OSH 88, phrases 1–2, rebarred

O   for a thou - sand tongues to   sing My great Re-deem-er's praise.

Ex. 61

1. The Christian Warfare, OSH 179, phrases 5–6, transposed and rebarred

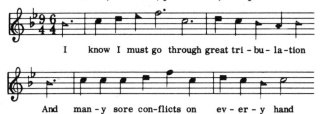

I know I must go through great tri - bu - la -tion

And man - y sore con-flicts on ev - er - y hand

2. An Address for All, SH 99, phrases 5–6, rebarred

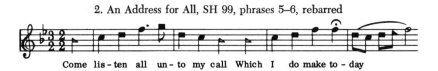

Come lis - ten all un - to my call Which I do make to - day

3. The Church's Desolation, OSH 89, phrases 5–6, rebarred

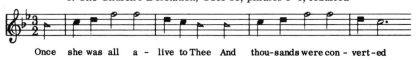

Once she was all a - live to Thee And thou-sands were con - vert -ed

4. Louisiana, OSH 207, phrases 5–6

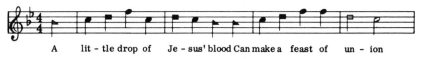

A lit - tle drop of Je - sus' blood Can make a feast of un - ion

5. Soda, NH 67, phrases 5–6, transposed

Un - num-ber'd com-forts to my soul Thy ten - der care be- stow'd

There are four examples in the second group (Ex. 62). Here phrase five begins on "fa" or "sol" and phrase six ends on "do" (if the line has six syllables) or "sol" (if the line has seven syllables).

In addition to all those in Ex. 62 the author found twenty-four examples in which two or more otherwise dissimilar tunes have a common phrase which is alike except for the pick-up note which serves as a connecting link from the preceding phrase (Ex. 63).

Ex. 62

1. The Converted Thief, SH 9, phrases 5–6, transposed and rebarred

His crimes with in- ward grief and shame The pen - i - tent con-fessed

2. Bound for Canaan, OSH 82, phrases 5–6, rebarred

I'm on my way to Ca - naan I'm on my way to Ca - naan

3. Christian Contemplation, NH 48, phrases 5–6

When shall I be de - li - vered From this vain world of sin

4. Hallelujah, OSH 146, phrases 5–6, transposed

And I'll sing Hal - le - lu - jah And you'll sing Hal - le - lu - jah

Ex. 63

1. Behold the Saviour, OSH 292, phrases 5 and last

To bleed and die for thee

Akers, OSH 293, phrases 4 and last

And wipe my weep-ing eyes

2. Bishop, OSH 420, phrase 4

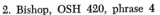

While all the an - gels sing

Sing On, OSH 381, phrase 8

Through all e - ter - ni - ty

3. Blooming Youth, OSH 176, phrase 2

In na - ture's smil - ing bloom

Lenox, SH 77, OSH 40, NH 42, phrase 2, transposed

The glad - ly sol - emn sound

4. Bozrah, SH 39, phrases 1, 5, and 7

Who is this that comes from far

New Orleans, SH 76, phrases 1 and 3, transposed

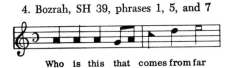

Why do we mourn de - part - ing friends

5. Deep Spring, NH 93, phrases 4 and 8   Pilgrim's Lot, SH 138, phrases 4 and 8

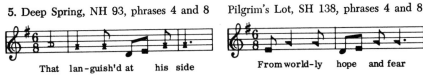

That lan - guish'd at his side   From world-ly hope and fear

Erie, NH 105, phrases 2, 4, and 8, transposed

And art thou pa - ci - fied

6. Florence, OSH 121, phrase 5

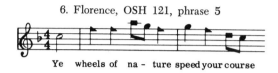

Ye wheels of na - ture speed your course

Weary Soul, OSH 72, phrase 5

Tho' chil-ling winds and beat-ing rains

7. Golden Hill, NH 81, phrase 2

I lift my— heart and voice

Sing On, OSH 381, phrase 6, transposed

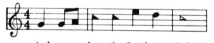

A - round the great white throne

8. Holy Manna, OSH 59, SH 103, NH 107, phrases 2, 4, and 8

And a - dore the Lord our God

Still Better, OSH 166, phrases 2, 4, and 8

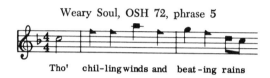

In the ser- vice of my Lord

9. Land of Rest, OSH 285, phrase 1, rebarred

O land of rest for thee I sigh

Restoration, OSH 271, phrase 1, rebarred

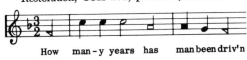

How man-y years has man been driv'n

10. Morning Trumpet, NH 99, SH 195, phrase 2

And reign with Him a - bove

Religion is a Fortune, OSH 319, phrase 2, transposed

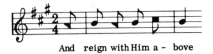

And reign with Him a - bove

11. Ninety-third, OSH 31, SH 7, NH 25, phrase 4

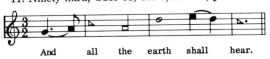

And all the earth shall hear.

New Year, NH 67, phrase 4, transposed

Is swift - ly rush - ing by.

12. Odem, OSH 295, phrase 4

With an in - vit - ing voice.

Bishop, OSH 420, phrase 4, transposed. The tunes are similar except for phrase 2.

While all   the   an - gels sing.

Sing On, OSH 381, phrase 8, transposed

And know as   we   are known.

13. Royal Proclamation, SH 146, phrase 1

Hear the roy - al pro-clam - a - tion,

Struggle On, OSH 400, phrase 1, transposed

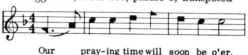

Our   pray-ing time will soon be o'er,

14. Spiritual Sailor, SH 41, phrase 5   Captain Kidd, SH 50, phrase 5

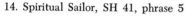

But   here a dis -mal o - cean,   The   grow-ing of the corn,

15. Sprague, SH 284, phrase 2   Stonington, SH 279, phrase 2

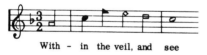   

With - in the veil, and   see   The   gos -pel trum-pet sounds,

16. Timmons, OSH 117, last phrase

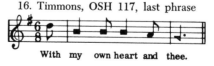

With my   own heart and thee.

We'll Soon be There, OSH 97, last phrase

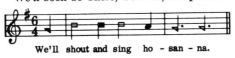

We'll shout and sing ho - san - na.

17. Ecstasy, OSH 106, phrase 4

Good Physician, SH 49, phrases 2 and 8

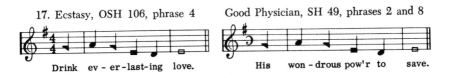

Drink ev - er - last - ing love.

His won - drous pow'r to save.

Save Mighty Lord, OSH 70, phrases 2, 4, and 7, transposed

Save might - y Lord

Detroit, SH 40, phrase 4

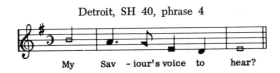

My Sav - iour's voice to hear?

Pilgrim, OSH 201, phrases 2, 4, and 8, transposed

But let us fol - low on.

18. Praise God, OSH 328, phrases 4 and last

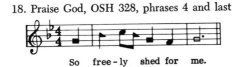

So free - ly shed for me.

Holy City, OSH 101, phrases 2, 4, and 8, transposed

And dwell with Him in light.

Messiah, OSH 131, phrases 2, 4, and 8, transposed

I   at   Thy   bar   ap - pear.

19. Good Physician, SH 49, phrases 1, 3, and 7

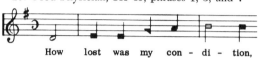

How   lost   was   my   con - di - tion,

Worlds Above, OSH 315, phrases 1 and 3, transposed

Lord   of   the world   a - bove,

20. Loving Kindness, OSH 275, phrases 2, 4, and 8

Hal - le, Hal - le - lu - jah.

Northport, OSH 324, phrases 4 and 8

Glo - ry! Hal - le - lu - jah!

21. Conversion, OSH 297, last phrase

The   grace ap - peared   so   great!

Webster, OSH 31, phrase 4, transposed

And   thus   sur - round   the   throne.

22. Timmons, OSH 117, last phrase

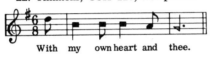

With   my   own heart and   thee.

We'll Soon be There, OSH 97, phrases 4 and 8

We'll shout   and   sing   Ho - san - na.

23. Child of Grace, OSH 77, phrases 2, 4, and 8

A   heaven pre-pared for   me.

Fiducia, SH 92, phrases 2, 4, and 8

Is   in - fi - nite de - light

24. Fiducia, SH 92, phrase 1

Fath - er   I   long   I   faint   to see

Star in the East, SH 16, phrase 1. Extended because of the text.

Hail   the blest morn   see   the   great Med - i - a - tor

Perhaps no. 24 should really have been included in this next group in which the pairs of phrases are similar but differ by a few notes (Ex. 64).

Ex. 64

1. Babe of Bethlehem, SH 78, phrase 5

To   roy - al   Jews   came   first   the   news

Repose, SH 151, phrase 5

To   sit   and   tell   Christ   loved   us   well

2. Beach Spring, OSH 81, phrases 2, 4, and 8, rebarred

Weak and   wound - ed   sick and   sore,

Devotion, OSH 48, phrases 1 and 4, transposed and rebarred

Like   Da - vid's harp   of   sol - emn sound.

3. Bozrah, SH 39, phrases 1, 5, and 7

Who   is   this   that comes from far,

Restoration, OSH 312, SH 5, phrase 2

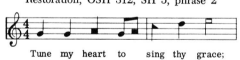

Tune   my   heart   to   sing thy   grace;

4. Deep Spring, NH 93, phrases 4 and 8

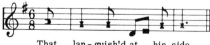

That   lan - guish'd at   his side.

Lovely Story, OSH 104, phrases 2, 4, and 8

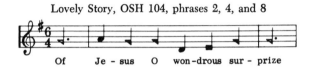

Of   Je - sus   O   won-drous sur - prize

5. Distress, SH 22, phrases 1 and 4, rebarred

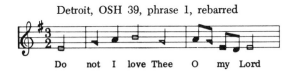

So   fades the love - ly   bloom - ing flow'r

Detroit, OSH 39, phrase 1, rebarred

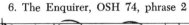

Do   not I love Thee   O   my Lord

6. The Enquirer, OSH 74, phrase 2

Or   to   de - fend   His cause

The Blessed Bible, OSH 347, phrase 2

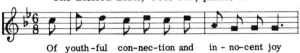

Of youth-ful con-nec-tion and in - no-cent joy

7. Ester, OSH 37, phrase 1

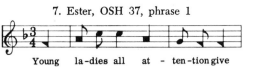

Young   la-dies all   at - ten -tion give

Restoration, OSH 271, phrase 1, rebarred

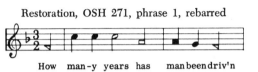

How man-y years has   man been driv'n

8. Greensborough, OSH 289, phrase 1

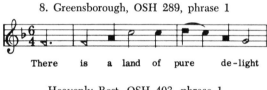

There   is   a   land   of   pure   de-light

Heavenly Rest, OSH 403, phrase 1

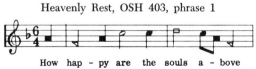

How hap - py are   the   souls   a - bove

9. Happiness, SH 40, phrase 1

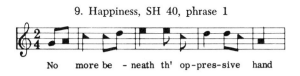

No   more be   - neath th' op-pres-sive   hand

Sincerity, SH 101, phrase 1, transposed

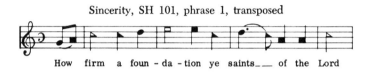

How   firm   a   foun - da -tion ye saints___ of the Lord

10. Idumea, OSH 47, SH 31, NH 44, phrase 1

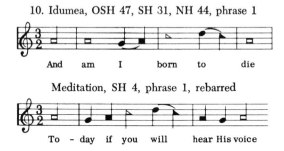

And   am   I   born   to   die

Meditation, SH 4, phrase 1, rebarred

To - day   if   you   will   hear His voice

11. Imandra, OSH 45, phrases 2–3

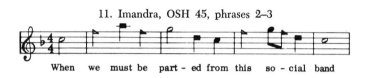

When   we   must be   part - ed from this   so - cial band

Highlands of Heaven, OSH 175, phrases 5–6 together, transposed

Where the bright bloom-ing flow'rs are their o - dor e - mit -ting

12. Liverpool, SH 1, phrase 1, rebarred

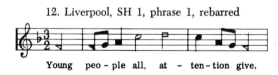

Young peo - ple all, at - ten-tion give,

Frozen Heart, OSH 93, phrase 1

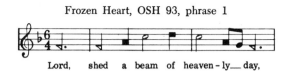

Lord, shed a beam of heaven - ly__ day,

13. Marietta, NH 90, phrase 1

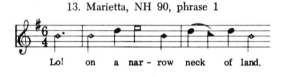

Lo! on a nar - row neck of land,

Christian's Delight, OSH 429, phrase 1, transposed

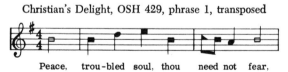

Peace, trou-bled soul, thou need not fear,

14. Marriage in the Skies, OSH 438, phrase 5

The might - y pen- nants of the skies

Timmons, OSH 117, phrase 1, transposed

Lord thou wilt hear me when I pray

15. Marriage in the Skies, OSH 438, phrase 3

The   glo - rious ju - bi - lee   is nigh

Timmons, OSH 117, phrase 5, transposed

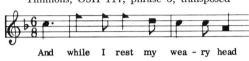

And   while   I   rest   my   wea - ry head

16. Martial Trumpet, SH 61, phrase 1, rebarred

Breth-ren don't you   hear the sound

Rockbridge, SH 288, phrase 1, transposed and rebarred

Life   is   the   time   to   serve the   Lord

17. Ninety-third, OSH 31, SH 7, NH 25, phrase 4

And   all   the   earth   shall   hear.

Prospect, OSH 30, phrase 2

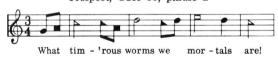

What   tim - 'rous worms we   mor - tals   are!

18. Sing to Me of Heaven, OSH 312, NH 73, phrase 4. NH is in the key of a minor.

To   waft   my soul   on   high.

Christian Soldier, NH 120, phrase 4, transposed from a minor

And mor - tal poi - sons grow;

19. Teacher's Farewell, OSH 34, phrase 3

How sad the thought to part with you;

Sing to Me of Heaven, OSH 312, NH 73, phrase 3, transposed

Sing songs of ho - ly ec - sta - cy,

20. Wayfaring Stranger, OSH 457, phrase 6

I'm go - ing there no more to roam;

Fellowship, OSH 330, phrase 2, transposed

Our hearts in Chris-tian love;

Horton, OSH 330, phrase 2

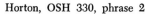

The pass - ing mo-ments say;

21. Old Ship of Zion, OSH 79, phrases 2 and 4

O glo - ry hal - le - lu - jah,

Lover of the Lord, OSH 124, phrase 2, transposed

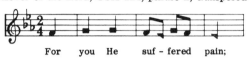

For   you   He   suf - fered   pain;

22. Primrose, OSH 47, SH 3, phrase 3, rebarred

A   sov'-reign balm   for   ev -'ry wound

Weeping Pilgrim, OSH 417, phrases 3 and 6, transposed

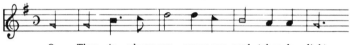

I'm   bound for Ca-naan's land.

23. Davis, SH 15, phrase 1

O   Thou in whose pre - sence my soul takes de - light

Redemption, SH 108, phrase 1

Hark hark glad   tid - ings   charm   our ears

24. Holy Army, NH 119, phrases 2 and 4

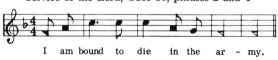

I   am bound to die   in His ar - my.

Service of the Lord, OSH 80, phrases 2 and 4

I   am bound to die   in the   ar - my.

25. Sincerity, SH 101, phrase 1

How firm a foun - da - tion ye saints of the Lord.

Happiness, SH 40, phrase 1, transposed

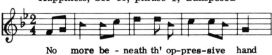

No more be - neath th' op-pres-sive hand

26. Sister's Farewell, OSH 55, phrase 5, rebarred

When I get home to that bright world

Resurrected, OSH 153, phrase 5

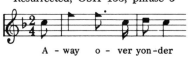

A - way o - ver yon -der

27. Timmons, OSH 117, phrase 5

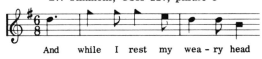

And while I rest my wea - ry head

Marriage in the Skies, OSH 438, phrase 7, transposed

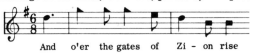

And o'er the gates of Zi - on rise

28. Wells, NH 19, OSH 28, SH 278, phrase 1, rebarred. OSH is in G.

Ye na - tions round the earth re - joice

Penick, OSH 387, phrase 1, rebarred

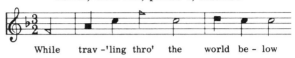

While   trav -'ling thro'   the   world be - low

29. Bradley, NH 38, phrase 1

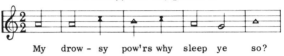

My   drow - sy   pow'rs why   sleep ye   so?

Loving Kindness, OSH 275, phrase 1

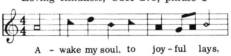

A   - wake my soul, to   joy - ful   lays,

30. Weeping Sinners, OSH 108, phrase 4

Bids   you His   sal - va - tion sing.

New Prospect, OSH 390, last phrase, transposed

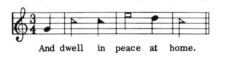

And dwell   in   peace   at   home.

31. Dying Minister, OSH 83, phrase 3

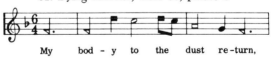

My   bod - y   to   the   dust   re -turn,

Frozen Heart, OSH 93, last phrase

This heart this fro -   zen heart   of mine.

There are doubtless many more examples of centonization in the three books. In fact, several more have been found since the above material was assembled.

One might speculate endlessly on the why of centonization. Some of the above phrases seem to be little more than stock cadence formulae, Ex. 63–5, for instance. Other instances are obviously the result of

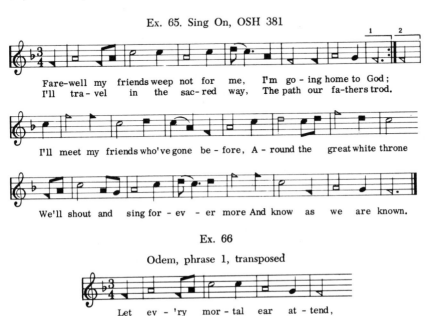

Ex. 65. Sing On, OSH 381

Fare-well my friends weep not for me, I'm go - ing home to God;
I'll tra - vel in the sac- red way, The path our fa-thers trod.

I'll meet my friends who've gone be - fore, A - round the great white throne

We'll shout and sing for - ev - er more And know as we are known.

Ex. 66

Odem, phrase 1, transposed

Let ev - 'ry mor - tal ear at - tend,

Bishop, phrase 1

Our Fa - ther's gone to that bright land,

like or similar words, such as Ex. 63–10 and Ex. 63–20. But further than this the author prefers not to commit herself.

In conclusion let us take a modern folk hymn and subject it to phrase and figure analysis. The tune chosen is "Sing On," OSH 381, by T. B. McGraw, dated 1935 (Ex. 65).

The first phrase seems to have been a favorite with the McGraw family, for a similar phrase occurs in "Odem," OSH 295, by Leon Mc-Graw, and the distinctive first figure is in "Bishop," OSH 420, again by T. B. McGraw (Ex. 66).

Phrase 2, except for the pick-up, is also the final phrase of "New Prospect," OSH 390, belonging to the "Deep Spring" group and attributed to W. S. Turner, 1866. Jackson gives the folk song background for "New Prospect" in SF 133, and its last phrase, together with the similar phrase from "Weeping Sinners," is quoted in Ex. 64–30. The first of the two middle phrases occurs in a different rhythm in "Newman," OSH 321. The latter is attributed to J. P. Rees and would therefore date from around the 1850s (Ex. 67).

Ex. 67. Newman, OSH 321, phrase 5

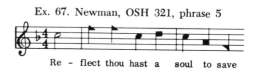

Re - flect thou hast a   soul   to save

Ex. 68. Resignation, SH 38, phrases 7–8. Phrases 2 and 4 are like phrase 8.

And   leads me   for His mer - cy's   sake In   paths of truth and grace.

The second middle phrase comes directly from "Golden Hill," NH 81, phrase 2, and has already been quoted in Ex. 63–7. The penultimate phrase begins like "Resignation," SH 38, and ends with a figure from "Sing On" itself, first phrase. The final phrase comes definitely from "Resignation," which Jackson comments upon in DE 94, and which can be found in manuals at least as early as 1832. It will be noted from Ex. 63-12 that "Bishop" and "Odem" have similar last phrases (Ex. 68).

I have no doubt that many another tune could be so analyzed.

VII

For my own part, I don't think myself confined to any rules
of composition laid down by any who went before me.

William Billings, Preface to *The Singing
Master's Assistant,* 3rd edition (1780)

꧁꧂꧁꧂

IT HAS BEEN mentioned before that the early singing school composers
may have been familiar with William Tans'ur's *Compleat Harmony* of
1736. This book contained an "Introduction to Practical Music" which
laid down certain rules for voice leading. Tans'ur, an Anglo-German of
doubtful musical training, evidently fancied himself as a theorist, for on
the title page of *The Royal Melody Compleat* of 1764 he styles himself
"Musico Theoretico."

How much did Tans'ur influence the singing school masters? Despite
Lowell Mason and John Tasker Howard, perhaps not so very much.[1] In
the first place, there is sheer Yankee pigheadedness as evidenced in the
Billings quotation above. In the second place, Tans'ur's rules are often
ambiguous even to a trained theorist. Take, for instance, Rule Three:
"Two fifths may be taken together, both rising and falling, if the one be
major and the other minor, (but not otherwise) the like is to be understood of fourths. Two of one kind may not pass together, by reason that
transposition of the parts in canon will render them fifths." One easily
sees that he is talking about a perfect to a diminished fifth, but what
about those words in parentheses? Does "and not otherwise" mean that
one may not have a diminished to a perfect fifth or that one may not
have two perfect fifths together? In context with the first part of the
rule it would seem to mean the former; in context with the last part it
would seem to mean the latter. Incidentally, this last part of the rule
seems to take for granted that music has a contrapuntal basis in which
a certain amount of imitation, with its consequent inversion, is inevitable.
It may be said now that this contrapuntal aspect was continued on in the
singing school tradition and survived in the harmonization of the folk
hymns.

1. Howard, p. 47.

Though Tans'ur gives no further rules governing consecutive fifths, a study of his music reveals that he allowed consecutive perfect fifths between what is evidently considered a passing tone and a chord tone (Ex. 69).

Ex. 69. Bromsgrove Tune, from *The Royal Melody Compleat*

Ex. 70. St. Martin's, *ibid.*

Ex. 71. Belford Tune, *ibid.*

In the case of consecutive octaves, Rule Eighteen bans them "in transition," which, from the illustration, seems to mean octaves in parallel motion occurring between the last of a group of eighth notes over a note of longer duration and the next change of harmony. Again, a study of his music reveals more than is covered by the rule. Consecutive octaves were obviously allowed if they were taken by contrary motion (Ex. 70).

Consecutive unisons (he seems not to have thought about these in inversion) obviously cause no concern, for they occur freely (Ex. 71).

Tans'ur also rules against hidden fifths and octaves.[2] But much more interesting are his model cadences. These are illustrated in both major and minor and are variations on the progression subdominant, dominant, and tonic with a supertonic sixth sometimes substituting for the subdominant. His music also shows the use of the tonic six-four and the Phrygian cadence. Indeed he seems to have been fond of the latter, for most of his minor hymns use this formula for one of the intermediate

Ex. 72. Bromsgrove Tune, *ibid.*, second phrase

Ex. 73. Belford Tune, *ibid.*

cadences. The particular voice leading that we associate with the Phrygian cadence always occurs between the bass and the tenor, for, of course, the tenor is the voice that carries the melody (Ex. 72). He also used the modulation to the dominant (Ex. 73).

Perhaps our first composers did study Tans'ur's rules; there is little actual evidence one way or the other. They did not use the Phrygian cadence; perhaps this is an indication that they didn't study the music, or perhaps they simply didn't like this type of cadence.[3] As

2. Rules 10, 14, 15.
3. This should not be taken too dogmatically. However, since the author failed to find a single instance of this cadence during the examination of a good many hymnals, it certainly is not common.

for the dominant-tonic cadence used by both Tans'ur and the Americans, this is the type of cadence most commonly heard in all types of European music of the day and the one easiest to sing, hear, and part write. It would have been common property with or without Tans'ur.

Whatever the influence, the American things are full of so-called consecutives, a circumstance that blasted them in the opinion of Lowell Mason and his nineteenth-century successors. Examples of these can be seen in the following:

1. Bridgewater. See *The Psalmodist's Companion* of 1793. Consecutive fifths appear in m. 4 and in the final cadence.
2. Calvary. Again in *The Psalmodist's Companion*. Consecutive fifths are to be found in m. 6 and consecutive unisons in m. 13.
3. China. See *The Musical Instructor* of 1818 and *The Beauties of Harmony* of 1814. There is a set of fifths between mm. 10 and 11.
4. Concord. See Holden's *Union Harmony*, 1793. There are consecutive octaves in m. 2.
5. The Rose of Sharon. See *The Singing Master's Assistant* of 1780 (3rd ed.). Both consecutive fifths and consecutive octaves occur in mm. 9 and 10 of the 6/8 section.

The above are only a few examples, chosen from a variety of composers without examining the chosen works too closely for further instances. Anyone interested can find a wealth of examples for himself. Let us concede that consecutives are to be found in the works of our first composers and go on from there—to cadences, for instance.

The works chosen for examination were the fifty-six examples of Early American work listed in Chapter II, omitting "Lisbon" which is not in anything like its original form, and "Amity" which for some reason the author failed to include when examining *The Beauties of Harmony*. Final cadences were examined in the early books where the remaining fifty-four examples were found. All had the bass progression of dominant to tonic; only three of these contained notes not in the dominant or dominant seventh spelling. The rest broke down into the following statistics:

1. Of the dominant chords: twenty-seven were complete triads, twelve were triads with no third, and six had no fifth. There were four complete dominant seventh chords and one dominant seventh with no fifth. Three of the dominant harmonies had notes outside the chord spelling.

2. Of the tonic chords: fourteen were complete triads, twenty-seven had no third, ten had no fifth, and two had only the roots present. No examples were found of tones outside the tonic spelling.

It is just possible that the preponderance of tonic chords without thirds in the final cadence was due to lack of part writing skill rather than any liking for the open sound of the root and fifth alone. As in the folk hymns, the final here is apt to be approached from above. The part writing of the authentic perfect cadence then requires the use of what generations of music students have learned to call Rule II: Give up the common tone and move the upper voices in the same direction (Ex. 74).

Ex. 74

Ex. 75. Bridgewater, from *The Psalmodist's Companion* (1793). The melody is of course in the tenor.

All theory teachers are familiar with the dismay this "rule" produces in students when they encounter it for the first time. After accepting the idea of "keeping the common tone" it is downright heresy suddenly to have to give it up. A few brighter students also discover the hidden fifths that are produced when the bass drops between the dominant and the tonic. Perhaps our early composers read their Tans'ur after all and tried to avoid this innocuous covered fifth. At any rate, it is interesting to note that when the final of the melody is approached from above, the final cadence is apt to look like Ex. 75. When the final is approached

from below, the final cadence is more apt to have a third in the tonic
(Ex. 76).

Except at the cadence points, there seems to have been no clear under-
standing of the principles of chord progression except perhaps in the
case of the sub-dominant, dominant, and tonic. But—and this is the

Ex. 76. Concord, *Union Harmony* (1793)

Ex. 77. Winter, *ibid.*

essential point—their harmony is triadic, and a vertical sampling of their harmony more often than not results in a triad spelling and occasionally a chord of the seventh. At least the chord usually can be built up in thirds (Ex. 77).

However, these early composers were often led into unconventional

Ex. 78. Montgomery, *ibid.*

Ex. 79. Easter Anthem, *New York Collection* (1794)

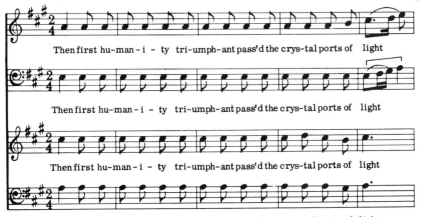

dissonances through an excessively linear viewpoint or a love of floridity. These dissonances, which frequently involve a second with some slower moving part, tend to come on the weak part of the beat (Ex. 78).

Billings' love of floridity caused him to fill in melodic thirds under practically all circumstances (Ex. 79).

One must always remember that these tunes were written to be sung; furthermore, they were to be sung without instrumental accompaniment. Consequently, composers made sure that each part was singable and interesting. Melodically, the individual parts are quite admirable and offer little difficulty to even an inexperienced singer. Melodic analysis of Billings "Rose of Sharon" gives the following incidence of intervallic relationships:

Major second, 45.5 per cent
Minor second, 22.54 per cent
Major third, 9.9 per cent
Minor third, 6.7 per cent
Perfect fourth, 9.9 per cent
Perfect fifth, 5.8 per cent
One instance each of the octave and the minor sixth.

Looking over other music of the period, this instance would seem to be generally typical. Augmented and diminished intervals are rare in a melodic line although they do occur occasionally. There is, for example, an augmented second in Billings' "Lament over Boston" in *The Singing Master's Assistant,* possibly used because of the nature of the text.

Chromaticism also is rare. Two instances occur in "Montague" by Timothy Swan: one is between phrases, the other occurs within the phrase.[4]

Everyone who has read John Tasker Howard's *Our American Music* is familiar with Tans'ur's directions for writing a fugue:[5]

> To compose a canon, you must first prick down your Fuge for such a Quantity of Notes as you would have to lead your point in *one* Part; and then carry the same Notes forward and prick them down in another Part, either in the Unision, 3rd, 4th, 5th, 6th, etc. above or below the Leading Part.
>
> A canon is a perpetual fuge, i.e. Parts always flying one before another; the following parts re-peating the very same Notes either

4. Quoted by Fisher, p. 37.
5. Howard, p. 56 (3rd ed.).

in Unison, or higher or lower as the leading Part, and because it is carried on by so strict a Rule, it is called a Canon, which is the superlative, or highest degree, of Musical Composition.

A single Fuge, or Imitation, is when Parts imitate one another.

A Double Fuge is when two or several Points, or Fuges fall in, one after the other.

As understood by Billings and his contemporaries, the "Fuge" turns out to be roughly similar to that of the sixteenth century; the voices were brought in one by one, an imitation of the first few notes being con-

Ex. 80. The Rose of Sharon, *The Singing Master's Assistant* (1778)

Ex. 81. Ocean, *The Beauties of Harmony* (1814)

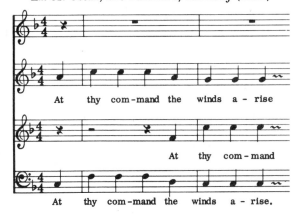

sidered sufficient, after which each voice might then proceed as suited the purpose of the composer. The first imitation is almost always at the octave or at the fifth, though quite often the third or the sixth would be used for one or another of the other two voices. The Americans seem also to have had a conception of the "tonal" answer, as Ex. 80 and 81 show.

The above does not pretend to be an exhaustive analysis of the style of our first composers. This has been done by others in some detail.[6] In general, however, the following should be kept in mind, particularly when reading the next chapter:

1. Though the writing is contrapuntal, a vertical analysis will reveal that the harmony is basically tertian; that is, the chords can be built up in thirds.
2. The inversions used are mostly root positions and first inversions, though there are apt to be more second inversions than is common in conventional harmony.
3. There are plenty of consecutive fifths and octaves, but each part is quite singable and is interesting in itself.
4. They used the harmonic minor and made frequent modulations to the dominant.
5. The final tonic frequently lacks a third.
6. Though there is little evidence that they understood the principles of chord progression, they did seem to understand the functions of tonic, subdominant, and dominant, particularly at cadence points.

The next point to consider is this: how have these old favorites survived the innumerable reprintings that preceded their appearance in the three books that form the basis of this study?

The answer is that, on the whole, they survived surprisingly well. One must, however, remember that shape-note manuals seldom print accidentals. In fact, one wonders if the compilers were really familiar with their functions. The following comes from the preface to the *New Harp of Columbia*: "A very popular error exists in the minds of many, who are not strangers altogether with music in regard to . . . the characters called flats and sharps. Many suppose that they affect the music, when the truth is, they serve no purpose but as signs of the key, and without which music in round notes would be a sealed book." At any rate, shape-note books almost never print the raised seventh of the scale in minor nor the raised fourth in making a modulation to the dominant. *The*

6. Barbour, for instance, in *The Church Music of William Billings.*

Original Sacred Harp does print an occasional accidental, but for the most part omits them.

A type of error is occasionally found which does not bother the singer of shaped notes but which is apt to be overlooked by the trained musician. This occurs when a shape is misplaced. An example is to be found in the OSH version of "Claremont": in m. 11 the shape of "la," belonging on A, has been misprinted on F. Other examples of this sort of thing occur in the following:

1. Easter Anthem, OSH 236, mm. 33–34. The shapes of sol-la-sol are printed a second too high.
2. Jubilee, SH 118. In m. 11 the shapes for sol and la are on D and E instead of on E and F.
3. Easter Anthem, OSH 236. In mm. 34-35, in the counter, the shapes for sol and la are on F and G instead of E and F.

There are doubtless many more of these misprints, and the analyst is warned to watch for them.

Another type of difference is to be found, especially in *The Original Sacred Harp*, when an early work is quite frankly said to be "re-arranged." Kimball's "Invitation" (OSH 327) is a good example. After "Jacob Kimboll, 1793" comes the further information "Re-arranged by Denson and James, 1911." The bass and tenor are reasonable facsimiles of earlier versions, but alto and soprano have many differences. Sometimes no arranger is given, but wide differences between earlier and later versions exist just the same. "Enfield" (OSH 184) and "Ninety-third" (NH 25) are two examples.

Generally speaking, the alto part is more apt to change over the years than any of the other parts. One reason is that some of the compositions were originally written in only three parts; another reason is that the alto is apt to be an uninteresting part and compilers may have padded the line a bit in order to attract singers. Tenor and bass lines are seldom changed very much.

If any reader is a choir director in the southern states with a yen for performing Early American music, he can use the Old Harp books, remembering to insert the correct accidentals, to note any misprints, and to avoid any number marked "re-arranged," and be assured of obtaining reasonable historic accuracy. If, on the other hand, the reader is a musicologist intent on a serious study of the harmonic practices of our forefathers, he is advised to study these numbers in their original forms if at all possible.

VIII

Why should fourths and fifths be the first intervals to appear in those documents that provide us with the evidence concerning the growth of European part-music?

Gustave Reese, *Music in the Middle Ages,* p. 250

It is rather that the development of polyphony seems spontaneously to have followed very similar paths in all parts of the world.

Ibid., p. 256

IT MIGHT be said also that polyphony tends to use the perfect intervals—the fourth, fifth, and octave—at a certain stage in the musical development of almost any people; and indeed Reese, quoting Schneider, goes on to make this clear.[1] The author, however, came to the study of the quartal harmony of the folk hymns not through organum, but through the theories of Joseph Yasser in *A Theory of Evolving Tonality.*

At the time the author was a graduate student at the Eastman School of Music. The *Theory* was a self-imposed holiday task, the first of a long list of books our hopeful instructors had advised us to read. The scene was a sunny garden and the time late August. The text was soporific, particularly to one whose mathematical background is practically nil. Suddenly there was a page of Chinese music, which, of course, one read as conscientiously as the text. It sounded vaguely familiar, and the reader was suddenly wide awake.

It sounded a little like Old Harp music.

To shorten this story, let us say that the first section of this treatise, on Infra-diatonic harmony, became a sort of Bible, and the remainder of this chapter describes the process by which the Yasser theories were applied to the folk hymns.

The following basic principles were assimilated:

1. The pentatonic scale seems to be the universal scale of primitive music.

1. *Music in the Middle Ages,* pp. 256, 257.

2. The logical basis for the harmonization of melodies based on this scale would be the dyad, a two-note chord formed by alternate notes of the pentatonic scale (Ex. 82).

Ex. 82

3. The use of dyads results normally in three-part harmony, just as the use of triads results in four-part harmony.
4. Although the fourth is the basic interval of harmonization, it is more normal to end on the "resonant" fifth than on the "irresonant" fourth. This is compared to the "acoustical amendment" of the Tierce de Picardie.[2]
5. Consecutive open fifths are not out of place in this style since they are inversions of the basic interval of harmonization.

These are the basic theories, illustrated in *A Theory of Evolving Tonality* by references to Chinese music as has been noted; in the later *Medieval Quartal Harmony* Yasser has shown how such a system might well have been applied to the harmonization of Gregorian chant.

It has already been noted that there are many pentatonic melodies among the folk hymns. Some of these have one or more of what Yasser terms "pien tones," that is "fa's" or "ti's" used non-harmonically. These tunes the author has elsewhere termed "basically pentatonic." There are also the true hexatonic melodies, which, as has been shown, the author considers to be pentatonic melodies in the process of becoming diatonic. If there is anything in the Yasser theories, it would be reasonable to suppose that they might apply to the pentatonic and basically pentatonic melodies in the Old Harp books as well as to Chinese music.

As a conscientious Eastmanite, the author first began with the cadences. A cadence, of course, is simply a stopping place, which either completes the musical thought (corresponding to a period in rhetoric) or interrupts it momentarily (as does the comma in a sentence). In music all voices employed lead naturally into this point of rest. The simplest cadences in two-part counterpoint in a diatonic major scale would be as shown in Ex. 83.

In the Ionian form of the pentatonic scale these cadences would be as shown in Ex. 84.

Since the melody is in the tenor of the Old Harp books, these two-

2. Joseph Yasser, *Medieval Quartal Harmony.*

part cadences, if they are present, should occur between the tenor and the bass. In none of the three books used in this study did one have to look far for examples. "Gospel Pool," OSH 34, has this final cadence, the second of the authentic cadences postulated (Ex. 85).

In *The Southern Harmony* the first of the simple dyadic cadences occurs in "Devotion," page 13, in the plagal form (Ex. 86).

Ex. 83

Authentic cadence   Plagal cadence

Ex. 84

Authentic cadence   Plagal cadence

Ex. 85   Ex. 86

The New Harp of Columbia has fewer folk hymns than either of the other two books, and the first dyadic cadence does not occur until page 43, in "Pleasant Hill" (Ex. 87).

These preliminary findings seemed to warrant a complete study of cadences, both final and intermediate, in the pentatonic and basically pentatonic tunes. For this purpose eighty of the Ionian tunes, all of the Aeolian, all of the Mixolydian, and all of the Dorian tunes were examined. About half of the cadences were unequivocally dyadic; they could be explained in quartal harmony but not in tertian.

The tabulation of the two-part cadences did not accept the following part writing between bass and tenor even though it is not inconsistent with the dyadic style. All tones belong to the pentatonic scale, but the voice leading firmly suggests dominant to tonic (Ex. 88).

Since the cadence in Ex. 88 is also the most common cadence in the work of Billings and other early composers, which show little dyadic evidence, the author prefers to think of it as an inheritance which has been absorbed into the basic pentatonic feeling, and let it go at that.

Ex. 87

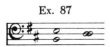

Ex. 88

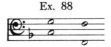

Ex. 89. Ninety-third Psalm, OSH 31,
final cadence

On   to___   God.

Ex. 90. Distress, OSH 32, final cadence

Made   to___ die.

One particular version of this cadence, however, seems to be something other than strictly tonal. The part writing involves a pair of perfect fifths between tenor and bass with a melody of mi-re-do (Ex. 89). Cadences using simple embellishments were accepted (Ex. 90).

In all the modes there are certain cadences that cannot be explained either in quartal or tertian harmony. This need not be wondered at in so primitive a style. Still other cadences, particularly those which involve a more complex use of pien-tones, may be analyzed in two or more different ways: these have been listed as "doubtful" in the following summary of the two-part cadences:

Mode	I	A	M	D
Number of cadences	517	191	94	50
Dyadic	272	103	62	23
Tonal	79	58	10	18
Octaves only[3]	58	14	0	3
Doubtful	22	9	5	1
Unexplained	55	7	17	5
Mi-re-do with fifths	28	0	0	0

3. This usually occurs as an intermediate cadence. For an example, see "Hebrew Children," OSH 133, phrase 4.

In all modes except the Mixolydian, the favorite dyadic cadence is the plagal form illustrated in Ex. 84. It is, of course, a dyad progressing to an octave. In the Mixolydian, where the final is always treated as the fifth of a major scale, the most common final cadence is shown in Ex. 91. Both dyads are in inversion.

Ex. 91. An Address for All, SH 99, final cadence

Hence a - way.

All possible combination of dyads, inversions, and octaves are used, as the following summary shows:

Mode	I	A	M	D
Dyad to dyad	15	4	3	0
Dyad to octave	81	27	2	5
Octave to dyad	8	3	5	1
Inversion to inversion	41	19	12	5
Inversion to octave	43	32	12	4
Octave to inversion	38	9	11	4
Dyad to inversion	24	7	14	2
Inversion to dyad	22	2	3	2

It has already been noted that three-part harmony is the logical basis for the quartal system. *The Southern Harmony* is indeed largely in three parts, but the other two books contain mostly four-part harmonizations. The explanation of this is that many of the older pentatonic hymns were originally written in three-part harmony (tenor, bass, and treble) and that altos were added later.[4] Throughout both *The Original Sacred Harp* and *The New Harp of Columbia* the legend "Alto (or counter) by. . ." occurs frequently. Because of the somewhat equivocal nature of the alto part we will not consider the four-part cadences.

Before any discussion of the three-part cadences, it would be wise to pause for a further consideration of what is and what is not consistent with the quartal style. We may expect many fourths and fifths in the harmonization since these are consonant intervals, and fewer thirds and sixths. Though the third is a dissonance, it is a very mild one since it

4. Jackson, *White Spirituals*, pp. 8, 96.

occurs as one of the basic dyads and is comparable to the triad on the leading tone in conventional tertian harmony. Like the leading tone triad it would not be suitable as a final harmony. An examination of the folk hymns chosen previously (some of which occur in slightly different harmonic versions in more than one book, making 317 in all) shows this to be borne out. Of the 317 hymns, 142 had final chords consisting of various arrangements of root and fifth, 31 had only the root in all voices, and in 89 four-part tunes the third appeared only in the alto, where it quite probably had been added later. The third appeared in the soprano in fifty-two more tunes.[5] Three others had tones other than those of the "tonic" chord, possibly as the result of an earlier misprint. Thus some 82 per cent of the harmonizations either avoided the third in the final chord or added it in the alto. It is only fair to remind the reader that this avoidance of the third in the final chord is also common in the Early American pieces.

In tertian harmony it is possible to add another third to a triad and form a chord of the seventh. In quartal harmony this procedure is also possible. The resulting three-tone sonorities in the Ionian mode of the pentatonic are shown in Ex. 92. For lack of a better term these will henceforth be referred to as "quartal sonorities."

Ex. 92

The three-part cadences are classified in the same way as the two-part cadences, except that they must be further organized according to the nature of the extra tone:

1. The cadence remains dyadic; that is, each of the two harmonies forming the cadence has one of the original notes doubled.
2. The cadence was dyadic in two parts, but the third part forms a quartal sonority.
3. The cadence could not be explained as two-part dyadic harmony, but the addition of the third part forms a quartal sonority.

Tonal cadences have been classified as to the thirds: (1) neither chord has a third; (2) there is a third in the first chord only; (3) there is a

5. New trebles are sometimes added as well. See "Ono," NH 62, which has a "New Treble, by M. L. Swan." The third is in the soprano here.

third in the second chord only; (4) both chords have thirds. The complete summary follows:

Mode	I	A	M	D
Dyadic in 3 parts	234	82	36	18
Dyadic in 2, quartal in 3 parts	53	20	18	2
Quartal sonority	73	13	10	6
Tonal with no third	43	2	0	12
Tonal with 3rd in first chord	7	32	3	4
Tonal with 3rd in second chord	25	4	4	0
Tonal with 3rds in both chords	7	5	0	0
Doubtful	11	17	1	1
Unexplained	60	16	22	7

Examples 93, 94, and 95 are typical of the first three types of cadences.

Apart from the cadence points, there seems to be no system of dyad progression; the harmony is purely intervallic and the writing definitely contrapuntal. As far as melodic writing is concerned, the procedures follow those of the Early Americans: each part makes a good melody, conjunct motion is more common than disjunct, and melodic skips tend to be small.

Ex. 93. Ester, OSH 37, final cadence. Dyadic in three parts. In this case the alto does not affect the character of the cadence.

The first of these points is quite evident to anyone who has ever sat down with an Old Harp book and done a little singing. The alto is the least interesting part for the very good reason that, as we have seen, it was frequently written after the other three which made good sense in themselves. The poor alto simply got what was left.

Ex. 94. Praise God, OSH 328, cadence in mm. 3–. Dyadic in two parts, quartal in three. The final note in the alto is outside the pentatonic scale.

Ex. 95. The Converted Thief, SH 9, cadence in mm. 7–8. Unexplained in two parts, the third part forms a quartal sonority. This one has only three parts.

As for the second of these points, an attempt was made to get some idea of the incidence of conjunct and disjunct motion in the individual parts. Ten tunes were chosen from all three books, representing all modes; these hymns were chosen for no particular reason other than that the author happened to like them. All except "Heavenly Armour" are listed in the Jackson books (see Appendix II for this tune), "Hopewell" being a slightly different form of "Columbus." They are:

1. An Address for All, SH 99, Mixolydian
2. The Good Old Way, SH 156, Ionian
3. The Good Physician, SH 49, Aeolian
4. Clamanda, OSH 42, Aeolian
5. Ester, OSH 37, Ionian
6. Jordan's Shore, OSH 50, Dorian
7. Weeping Pilgrim, OSH 417, Mixolydian

    8. Heavenly Armour, NH 56, Mixolydian
    9. Hopewell, NH 37, Aeolian
  10. Deep Spring, NH 93, Ionian

In these hymns, which may be taken as typical, the proportion of conjunct and disjunct motion by parts is as follows:

Part	Conjunct Motion	Disjunct Motion
Soprano	83%	16%
Alto if present	82%	17%
Tenor	84%	15%
Bass	80%	19%

These percentages are admittedly rough and by no means worked out to the last decimal. The 1 per cent discrepancy in each part represents the approximate incidence of repeated notes.

As to the intervals used melodically a similar rough count runs as follows:

Interval	S	A	T	B
3rds	78%	56%	76%	64%
4ths	20%	36%	16%	21%
5ths	1.5%	5%	6%	11%
6ths	.05%	2%	1%	3%
octaves	0	0	1%	1%

Again, the above figures are not to be taken as gospel; they are intended merely to show what intervals predominate in the melodic line. For those acquainted with the Yasser writings it may be said that these intervals are thought of conventionally: a third is counted diatonically, not as a second in the pentatonic scale.

Harmonically the hymns are much more individual. Three main principles emerge from an analysis. (1) Vertical consonances are the fourth, fifth, unison, and octave. (2) Thirds and sixths are treated very much as dissonances are treated in traditional tertian harmony; they are "prepared" and "resolved." (3) Non-harmonic tones are quite common and are used much as they are in conventional harmony. The passing tone, neighboring tone, appoggiatura, escape tone, changing tone, and suspension appear in this order of frequency. Unlike conventional harmony, the suspension is quite rare.

That fourths, fifths, unisons, and octaves are numerous in these harmonizations may be clearly seen from the following table. The same ten tunes were used.

Hymn	Bass to tenor			Bass to alto		
	4,5,1,8	3,6	2,7	4,5,1,8	3,6	2,7
1.	32	10	0			
2.	47	10	0			
3.	43	9	0			
4.	56	2	2	44	8	3
5.	32	0	0	20	10	2
6.	32	12	8	28	18	5
7.	28	20	0	Alto added later		
8.	26	6	0			
9.	45	6	4	37	8	7
10.	35	6	0	24	7	0

Hymn	Bass to soprano		
	4,5,1,8	3,6	2,7
1.	25	15	2
2.	46	9	2
3.	37	14	1
4.	53	7	3
5.	22	8	2
6.	34	13	4
7.	22	21	5
8.	21	11	0
9.	42	6	4
10.	22	8	2

It will be noticed that the proportion of perfect intervals varies widely in the individual hymns, from the bass and tenor of "Ester" (no. 5) where nothing but perfect intervals are used, to the bass and soprano of "Weeping Pilgrim" (no. 7), the only instance where imperfect intervals outnumber perfect ones. Parenthetically, the bass and tenor of "Arbour" (NH 90), which consists only of perfect fifths in the opening four measures, might well be quoted here. "Arbour," though by singing school master M. L. Swan, is not included in the list of folk hymns, since it is more or less a fuguing piece (Ex. 96).

It has already been said that thirds and sixths seem to be treated as dissonances. The procedures governing their approach (their "preparation") may be summarized thus:

1. A third or sixth may be used harmonically if one member is held as a common tone from the preceding chord.

2. Less frequently a third or sixth may be "prepared by substitution"; that is, one tone of the interval will be in the preceding chord but in a different voice.

3. The third or sixth may be approached in contrary motion in the two parts involved.

4. One member of the third or sixth may appear in a third part if two other voices are moving in contrary motion, particularly if one of these voices doubles one of the interval members.

Ex. 96. Arbour, NH 90, mm. 1–4, bass and tenor only

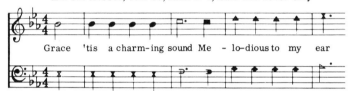

Ex. 97. An Address for All, SH 99, mm. 1-10, rebarred

5. Thirds and sixths sometimes appear as passing tones in parallel motion, particularly if one member is a pien-tone. In this case the first third or sixth will be prepared.

Ex. 98. Weeping Pilgrim, OSH 417, mm. 4-6. Note also the "preparation" of the thirds and sixths.

them - I'm a   poor   mourn-ing Pil - grim

Ex. 99. Deep Spring, NH 93, m. 6. The G in the soprano, forming a third with the bass, is unprepared.

on   a   wretch

All of the above practices are illustrated in the three-part hymn "An Address for All" (Ex. 97).

A laborious count of all the thirds and sixths in the ten hymns used for detailed analysis revealed that 94.2 per cent of them were prepared in one of the above five ways. This number breaks down into the following:

Around 30.4 per cent were prepared by the first method.
Around 11.9 per cent were prepared by the second method.
Around 35.2 per cent were prepared by the third method.
Around 8.1 per cent were prepared by the fourth method.
Around 8.6 per cent were prepared by the fifth method.
Around 6 per cent were unprepared in any way.

Ex. 100. The Good Old Way, SH 156, mm. 10–12

Ex. 101. The Good Old Way, SH 156, mm. 8–9

Ex. 102. Ester, OSH 37, mm. 3–4

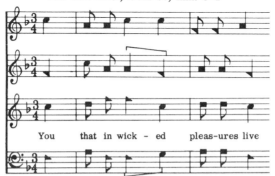

Thirds and sixths usually resolve very simply into a dyad or its inversion or into an octave. This accounts for slightly over 67 per cent of the resolutions. The resolution of both the third and the sixth into an inverted dyad may be seen in Ex. 98.

The resolution of a third to an octave is illustrated in Ex. 99.

"The Good Old Way" (SH 156) illustrates the resolution of a sixth to a dyad and offers as well a further example of the resolution of a third to an octave (Ex. 100).

Sometimes the third or sixth may be separated from its resolution by another third or sixth (or more rarely another interval), one of whose members is a pien-tone (Ex. 101). This might be compared to the "ornamental" resolution of conventional harmony. This occurred in approximately 13 per cent of the instances.

Ex. 103. Hopewell, NH 37, m. 1

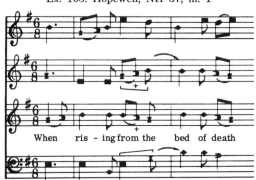

When   ris - ing from the   bed of death

Quite rarely (about 2 per cent of the time) a third or a sixth resolves into two tones that form part of a three-tone quartal sonority, as in Ex. 102.

At this point a word should be said about the third that occurs as one of the basic dyads between "do" and "mi." As has been mentioned before in this chapter, this third may be likened to the triad on the leading tone in conventional theory; in fact, Yasser terms this third a "diminished dyad."[6] It of course becomes a sixth on inversion. Most of the time it is approached and left like any other third or sixth, yet it seems sometimes to be of a little more importance. It may, for instance, serve as the resolution of another third or sixth, but only if one of its members is present in the preceding interval. This occurred nearly 10 per cent of the time

6. *Theory*, p. 77.

in the hymns examined. The diminished dyad then resolves as any other third or sixth. Example 103 illustrates the practice.

The matter of non-harmonic tones may be summed up briefly by a quotation from Yasser's *Medieval Quartal Harmony*: ". . . their fundamental technique is virtually the same as that in the tertian system, even though the chords themselves are different."[7]

Ex. 104. Carnsville, OSH 109, m. 5. A passing tone in the pentatonic scale (the alto was added later).

Ex. 105. Columbiana, OSH 56, m. 3. A neighboring tone in the pentatonic scale.

By far the most important non-harmonic tones in the Old Harps, as indeed in almost any other style of music, are the passing tones and the neighboring tones. Both occur in all voices, may progress up or down, and may be of two kinds: members of the pentatonic scale or pien-tones. Both occur usually as unaccented non-harmonic tones, although both do

7. Page 74.

occasionally occur on the accent. Only rarely does the unaccented passing tone or neighboring tone carry a syllable of the text.

Single unaccented passing tones or neighboring tones are used in a
perfectly straightforward manner and are easily recognized. Examples
104 and 105 illustrate the use when the non-harmonic tone is a member
of the pentatonic scale.

The unsupported pien-tone neighboring tone is extremely rare. Single

Ex. 106. Charlestown, OSH 52, m. 5

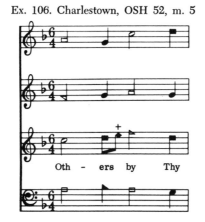

Oth - ers by Thy

Ex. 107. The Christian or Carnsville, SH 26, mm. 13–14

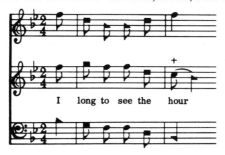

I long to see the hour

passing tones are more apt to be members of the pentatonic scale,
though the pien-tone passing tone does occur (Ex. 106).

Accented single passing tones frequently form a syncopation near an
important cadence (Ex. 107).

A pien-tone dissonance is apt to be supported by a non-harmonic
tone in another voice that makes a third or sixth with it. A third voice
may do various things: it may double the pien-tone in contrary motion,
it may double the supporting tone, it may double either of the other

lines in octaves, or it may add a different tone that usually makes some sort of quartal harmony with the supporting tone. Note that in each of Ex. 108–14 the third or sixth formed by the pien-tone resolves normally.

If the pien-tone is doubled, this is apt to take place either in the soprano or in the alto, where, of course, it may have been added later.

Ex. 108. Idumea, SH 31, m. 7. The third voice doubles the pien-tone in contrary motion, and the resolution is a quartal sonority.

Ex. 109. The Good Old Way, SH 156, mm. 3–4. The third voice doubles the supporting tone, and the resolution is an inverted dyad.

Ex. 110. Columbus, SH 55, mm. 1–2. Same doubling, but the resolution is the diminished dyad.

Ex. 111. Louisiana, SH 62, mm. 13–14. Same doubling, but the resolution is a quartal sonority. In this case, it happens also to make a triad.

Ex. 112. Heavenly Armour, NH 56, mm. 8–9. Same as the above except that the pien-tone is a neighboring tone.

Ex. 113. Prospect, SH 92, mm. 5–8. The supporting line is doubled in octaves, and the resolution is to the diminished dyad.

One instance of the pien-tone doubled in the soprano is in Ex. 108, another in Ex. 115.

It will be remembered that in Ex. 111 the chord of resolution was a quartal sonority which, in more conventional terms, was also a triad. This frequently happens when the third voice forms a dyad or an inversion of a dyad with the supporting voice. The tone in the third voice may be either non-harmonic or harmonic. This is illustrated in Ex. 116, which is really a further example of pien-tone doubling.

Double pentatonic passing tones are almost always unaccented. When they move in contrary motion, they may form almost any interval possible in the pentatonic scale. Note Ex. 117–20.

Ex. 114. Parting Hand, SH 113, m. 1. Same doubling, but the resolution is to an octave.

Ex. 115. Cuba, OSH 401, mm. 1–4. Since the alto to this was added fifty-two years later, the resolution may safely be considered a dyad in root position.

Double pentatonic passing tones in parallel motion occur most frequently as fourths. One of the lines may be doubled in octaves (Ex. 121, 122).

Anticipations are fairly rare. They occur only as notes of the pentatonic scale, on half beats, and do not carry a syllable of the text. As in other styles, they occur usually in the cadence (Ex. 123, 124).

Ex. 116. Primrose, OSH 47, mm. 6–7. The doubled line is in the alto. These measures, copied exactly from OSH, include one of the misprints mentioned earlier. The first note of the soprano, though the shape is correct, should be on C, not D.

Ex. 117. Day of Judgment, SH 84, mm. 10–11. The passing tones form the interval of a fifth. Notice also the pien-tone passing tone in the last measure. It resolves to an unmistakable quartal sonority.

Ex. 118. Judgment, SH 47, m. 10. The passing tones form the interval of a fourth.

Ex. 119. Idumea, NH 44, mm. 8–9. The passing tones form the interval of a ninth.

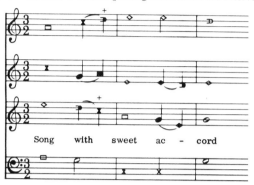

Ex. 120. Holy Manna, SH 103, m. 2. The passing tones form the interval of an octave.

Ex. 121. Sweet Rivers, OSH 61, mm. 13–14. The fourth is between bass and tenor; the soprano doubles the tenor.

Ex. 122. Prospect, OSH 30, m. 1. The fourth is between the tenor and soprano; the bass doubles the tenor.

Ex. 123. Golden Hill, NH 81, mm. 2–3, 12–13. These are both cadences.

Ex. 124. Done with the World, OSH 88, m. 3. First cadence.

Ex. 125. Prospect, SH 92, mm. 9–10

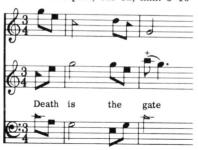

Ex. 126. Contented Soldier, SH 314, mm. 9–11

Ex. 127. Bower of Prayer, SH 70, m. 15

Appoggiaturi occur both on notes of the pentatonic scale and on pien-tones. The former are rare and occur on strong beats in half-beat note values. They do not carry a syllable of the text (Ex. 125, 126).

Pien-tone appoggiaturi occur on the syllable "fa" on both full-beat and half-beat note values. Except for one important idiom they carry no syllable of the text (Ex. 127, 128).

Ex. 128. Exultation, SH 88, mm. 1–3

Come a - way to the skies my be - lov - ed

Ex. 129. Hallelujah, OSH 146, mm. 3–6

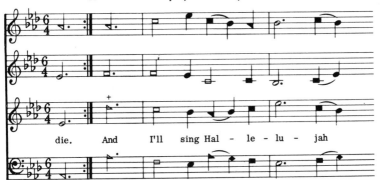

die. And I'll sing Hal - le - lu - jah

Ex. 130. Converted Thief, SH 9, mm. 8–10

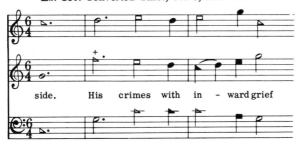

side. His crimes with in - ward grief

The idiom mentioned occurs in certain Mixolydian tunes at the beginning of the second section. It involves a skip of a seventh up to "fa," which may be harmonized either with "do" or with "sol." The appoggia-tura occupies half of the measure and carries a syllable (Ex. 129, 130).

The escape tone occurs in the cadence as a part of the melodic formula "re-mi-do." The formula is quite common in other styles of course. When the escape tone device is used in the Old Harps, the "mi" occurs on the last half beat of the measure and does not share the harmony of the preceding chord, though they may have the same bass note (Ex. 131).

Ex. 131. Ragan, OSH 176, m. 9. The alto, added forty-two years after the compo-sition of the hymn, is omitted.

Ex. 132. Holy Manna, SH 103, mm. 7–8. Cadential 9–8 suspension with ornamenta-tion.

Suspensions may occur at the cadence or within the phrase; they occur only in the upper voices. Two varieties are possible, the 9–8 and 6–5. The traditional variations of ornamentation and change of bass under the resolution are possible in this style also (Ex. 132, 133).

All of the non-harmonic tones may be combined with one another in hymns with three or four parts. In Ex. 132 a lower pentatonic neighbor tone appeared with the ornament to the suspension. Nine times out of ten a pien-tone will form a third or a sixth with one of the other lines. Two typical instances are shown in Ex. 134 and 135.

It is highly improbable that the composers of the folk hymns had any

Ex. 133. Happiness, SH 40, mm. 3–4. 6–5 suspension ornamented and with a change of bass. The D marked [?] is a rare 7–6 suspension. Note that it occurs in the inverted diminished dyad.

'neath   th' op - pres - sive   hand

Ex. 134. Cleburne, OSH 314, mm. 7–8

And   crown   Him   Lord   of   all.

Ex. 135. Dying Minister, OSH 83, mm. 1–2

The   time   is   swift - ly

of the above principles gathered together in any sort of compendium, written or oral, for their guidance. There are too many exceptions, too many places that are inexplicable. Nevertheless, through all of the penta-tonic and even the hexatonic tunes there is a hard core of quartal harmony, sonorities that can be explained only by accepting the basic Yasser theories.

Incidentally, it is amusing to note that the singing masters did not in practice accept the rules so cheerfully laid down in the "Rudiments of Music" section that opens each of the three manuals. Both Swan and Walker classify the third and sixth as concords, and *The Original Sacred Harp* comes out squarely for tertian harmony in Chapter vii of the "Rudi-ments of Music." The following passages might well have been taken from any mid-nineteenth-century book on harmony:[8]

> 2. Chords. A chord is formed by taking any tone of the scale as the fundamental, or tonic [sic] and adding its third and fifth or their octaves, always counting upward. The chords thus formed are named from the harmony names of the tones from which they originate, as follows:

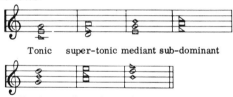

> Tonic   super-tonic mediant sub-dominant
>
> Dominant sub-mediant sub-tonic

The Original Sacred Harp also prohibits consecutive fifths and octaves: "7. Consecutives. Two parts moving up or down a perfect fifth apart give the effect of two keys and should be avoided. Two parts moving up or down a perfect Prime or a perfect Octave apart produce a weak effect and should be avoided."

Perhaps the composers and arrangers of the Old Harps were as rug-gedly individualistic as William Billings, whose feelings on the matter were quoted in Chapter vii. More likely, however, they were actuated by that innate harmonic sense which Yasser says " . . . is one of the most powerful driving forces in the evolution of music."[9] If the perfect fourth and fifth are indeed the natural intervals of harmonization in pentatonic melodies, then these hymns are exactly what one might expect from un-trained but essentially musical people.

8. Page 21.
9. *Medieval Quartal Harmony*, p. 9.

IX

There's a lot of good Gospel in that there song.

Singer at an Old Harp Meeting, East
Maryville Baptist Church, Maryville,
Tennessee, April, 1950

T HE SPEAKER was an elderly country woman who sat next to me in the counter section. Dressed neatly and even stylishly in flowered rayon, she had the sweetest smile I have ever seen. She was also deeply serious.

The texts of the Old Harps do contain a lot of good gospel; they also contain a lot of Old Testament ideas. If many of the texts reflect more of the wrath of an angry God than the mercy of a gentle Saviour, it is because they date from the seventeenth and eighteenth centuries when the evangelistic sects preached hell-fire and damnation to those not experiencing an agonizing conversion.

Though the texts would doubtless prove interesting to a student of theology as relics of the two Great Awakenings, the author is no theologian. This chapter, therefore, proposes to deal rather superficially with the origins of the texts and then go on to the musical settings.

It was mentioned in Chapter II that many of the anthems of Early America had Scriptural texts. The "Easter Anthem" of Billings, while not entirely Scriptural, quotes from I Corinthians 15:20. Billings' "Rose of Sharon" takes its text, by direct quotation, from Song of Solomon 2:1-4 and 7-11. "David's Lamentation," in the first eight measures, is a free adaptation of II Samuel 18:33, first half; the rest of the anthem quotes directly from the same verse. "Funeral Anthem" quotes from Revelation 14:13, while "Heavenly Vision" incorporates words from Revelation 7:9, 5:11, 4:8, and 8:13.

By far more common are the metrical versions of the Psalms, particularly those by Isaac Watts. Dr. Watts wrote original texts as well; in fact he is responsible, in the folk hymns alone, for twenty-seven texts, many of which are used for more than one tune. Charles Wesley is responsible for twelve texts in the three books and John Newton for seven, while assorted other eighteenth-century writers account for twenty-three more.

117

Earlier texts include the anonymous "Jerusalem my Happy Home," John Gambold's translation of a German pietistic hymn "O Tell me no More of this World's Vain Store," and a lovely translation of the Nicolai chorale "How Brightly Shines the Morning Star." There are, of course, many texts by humbler poets, some of which will be mentioned later. In general, however, the texts warn of the shortness of life, the anxiety for salvation, and the hope of heaven. Consider the following:

> The watchmen blow the trumpet round
> Come listen to the solemn sound
> And be assured there's danger nigh
> How many are prepared to die?
>
> (The Watchman's Call, SH 65)

> Broad is the road that leads to death
> And thousands walk together there
> But Wisdom shows a narrow path
> With here and there a traveller.
>
> (Windham, SH 48)

> Now in the heat of youthful blood
> Remember your Creator, God.
> Behold the months are hastening on
> When you shall say, my joys are gone.
>
> (Exhortation, OSH 272)

> And now my friends both old and young
> I hope in Christ you'll still go on
> And if on earth we meet no more
> O may we meet on Canaan's shore.
>
> (Farewell to All, OSH 69)

Besides the Scriptural and doctrinal texts there are many that are patriotic, most of which would seem to be of early origin:

> No more beneath th' oppressive hand
> Of tyranny we mourn.
> Behold a smiling, happy land
> Which Freedom calls her own.
>
> (Happiness, SH 40)

The text of "The American Star" (OSH 346) commemorates Washington and two other heroes of the Revolution, Dr. Warren who lost his life so bravely at Bunker Hill, and Richard Montgomery who fell at Quebec:

The spirits of Washington, Warren, Montgomery
Look down from the clouds with bright aspect serene
Come soldiers, a tear and a toast to their memory
Rejoicing they'll see us as once they have been.
To us the high boon by the gods have been granted
To spread the glad tidings of liberty far.
Let millions invade us, we'll meet them undaunted
And conquer or die by the American Star.

"The Ode on Science," NH 208, recalls that both the British and the French were once our enemies:

The British Yoke, the Gallic chain
Was urged upon our neck in vain
All haughty tyrants we disdain
And cry, long live America!

Some texts are true religious ballads. That of "The Romish Lady," SH 82, is a real ballad text and is often sung in other than Old Harp circles. Dr. Jackson thinks it dates from Inquisition times.[1] It goes on for eleven verses and ends with the martyrdom of the Romish Lady, brought up in popery. "The Babe of Bethlehem," SH 78, tells the story of the Nativity. "Missionary Farewell," SH 328, is exactly that, for six stanzas. Other religious ballads and their subjects, are as follows:

1. "The Midnight Cry," SH 32, NH 84. The wise and foolish virgins. Ten stanzas.
2. "The Sufferings of Christ," SH 85. The Crucifixion. Eight stanzas.
3. "Edmonds," OSH 115. The creation, duties, and rights of woman. Thirteen stanzas.
4. "Humility," NH 112, and "The Converted Thief," SH 9, OSH 44. The thief on the Cross. Six stanzas.

Among the most interesting texts are those with refrains and interpolations; according to Charles A. Johnson these are the result of camp meeting influence.[2] Any text may be treated this way, with the refrain varying from a simple "Hallelujah" to something relatively complex, such

1. *Spiritual Folk-Songs*, no. 1.
2. *The Frontier Campmeeting: Religion's Harvest Time*, pp. 201 ff.

as "And I don't expect to stay much longer here." Frequently the basic text is one of the older English texts mentioned earlier in this chapter. For example, the Charles Wesley hymn beginning "He comes, He comes, the Judge severe" gets a refrain of "Halle, hallelujah" after each line, thus:

> He comes, He comes, the Judge severe
> Halle, hallelujah!
> The seventh trumpet speaks Him near
> Halle, hallelujah!
> His lightening flash and thunder roll
> Halle, hallelujah!
> How welcome to the faithful soul
> Halle, hallelujah![3]

Closely allied to this is another type of refrain in which each of the first two lines is followed by the customary refrain, these being followed by the interpolation of a chorus of new material which itself ends with the refrain. Thus the Wesley hymn just quoted becomes the following:

> He comes, He comes the Judge severe
> Roll, Jordan, roll
> The seventh trumpet speaks Him near
> Roll, Jordan, roll.
> I want to go to heaven, I do
> Hallelujah, Lord
> We'll praise the Lord in heaven above
> Roll, Jordan, roll.[4]

A third type of text omits the refrain in the chorus of new material. This chorus is usually characterized by a certain amount of repetition. Watts' hymn that he called "Christ's Presence Makes Death Easy" thus gets a chorus whose literary style is somewhat at variance with the original:

> Why should we start and fear to die?
> What tim'rous worms we mortals are!
> Death is the gate of endless joy
> And yet we dread to enter there.

Chorus:

3. "Hallelujah," SH 139.
4. "Roll Jordan," OSH 274.

Roll on, roll on, sweet moments roll on
And let the poor pilgrim go home, go home.[5]

There are a few items in *The Original Sacred Harp* that are unmistakably songs of invitation for use in camp meetings or possibly revival meetings. These are remarkable for the possibility of almost endless verses, to be continued until the last mourner has reached the bench. In "Cuba," OSH 401, preachers, fathers, and mothers successively "Tell it to the world, poor mourner's found a home at last." Presumably brothers, sisters, and children might also be called upon if the need arose. Other songs of this type are "Jester," OSH 331; "Resurrected," OSH 153; "Rocky Road," OSH 294; and "Weeping Pilgrim," OSH 417.

A knowledge of traditional texts seems to be necessary for an Old Harp composer. The coupling of refrains and choruses to much older texts suggests this, as does the fact that a given text need not be associated with any one tune. A typical text is by the American John Leland. Leland, a Baptist evangelist who lived between 1754 and 1841, is further noted for the fact he journied from Cheshire, Massachusetts, to Washington to present an enormous cheese to President Jefferson on New Year's Day, 1802.[6] The hymn has twelve stanzas, the first two of which are quoted here:

O when shall I see Jesus
And reign with Him above
And from the flowing fountain
Drink everlasting love?

When shall I be delivered
From this vain world of sin
And from my blessed Jesus
Drink endless pleasures in?

The text is used, either in its entirety or in parts, for no less than five tunes in *The Original Sacred Harp*, four in *The Southern Harmony*, and three in *The New Harp of Columbia*. "Mutual Love," OSH 410, SH 53, and "Faithful Soldier," SH 122, NH 48 (in the latter it is called "Christian Contemplation"), present the text without refrain or chorus. In "Bound for Canaan," OSH 82, SH 193, the chorus is:

5. "Roll On," OSH 275.
6. L. H. Butterfield, "Elder John Leland, Jeffersonian Itinerant," *Proceedings of the American Antiquarian Society*, Vol. 62, Pt. 2 (October 15, 1952).

I'm on my way to Canaan
I'm on my way to Canaan
I'm on my way to Canaan
To the New Jerusalem.

In "Morning Trumpet," OSH 85, SH 195, NH 99, there occur both refrain and chorus: the refrain "And shall hear the trumpet sound in that
morning," and the chorus "Shout O glory, for I shall mount above
the skies / And shall hear the trumpet sound in that morning."

"Ecstasy," OSH 106, adds a chorus after each stanza: "O had I wings,
I would fly away and be at rest / And I'd praise God in His bright
abode."

"Religion is a Fortune," OSH 319, again has both refrain and chorus;
the former is a simple "Shout glory halle, hallelujah," and the latter,

When we all get to heaven
We will shout aloud and sing
Shout glory halle, hallelujah.

Another favorite text is the Samuel Stinnet hymn "On Jordan's Stormy
Banks I Stand," which was included in Dr. Ripon's famous *Collection*
of 1787. (The adjective was "rugged" in that version.) It is used thirteen
times in the three books, sometimes with refrains, choruses, or both,
sometimes for fuguing pieces. Sometimes it is used with a straightforward
presentation of the text. For good measure, "McKay," OSH 433, a
fuguing piece, uses only the second verse.

While most of the verse forms fall into the meters common to the
average hymnal, one rather uncommon verse form should be noted. This
is the "Captain Kidd" form from the hymn of the same name in *The
Southern Harmony.*[7]

Through all the world below
God is seen all around
Search hills and valleys round
There He's found.
The growing of the corn
The lily and the thorn
The pleasant and forlorn
All declare God is there
In the meadows dressed in green
There He's seen.

7. See the examples in Chapter IV.

Other hymns which have somewhat the same meter and the same stanza form are "Wondrous Love," OSH 159, SH 252, NH 143, beginning "What wondrous love is this /O my soul, O my soul," and another is "Solemn Thought," SH 29. The thought is certainly solemn enough:

Remember sinful youth
You must die, you must die.
Remember sinful youth
You must die.

Later additions to *The Original Sacred Harp* tend to rely on tried-and-true texts. Thus "Infinite Day" by Mrs. Ruth Denson-Edwards, page 446 in the 1936 edition, has a text by Isaac Watts, while "Wondrous Cross" by Paine Denson on the next page uses the familiar "When I survey the wondrous Cross." It was written in 1932 and "Infinite Day" in 1936. In the 1960 edition the added songs show more of a tendency to use newly composed texts, but Charles Wesley and Isaac Watts are still well represented.

The poetic meters of the hymns vary. That of "Happiness," the fifth text quoted in this chapter, is in Common Meter; that is, it is iambic, with eight syllables in the first line, six in the second, eight in the third, and six in the fourth. "The American Star" is anapaestic, with a syllable pattern of 12.11. "Ode on Science" is in Long Meter: iambic, with eight syllables in all lines. All of the above illustrations begin on the unaccented syllables; meters of the 8.7 or 7.7 variety usually begin on accented syllables, as in the following:

Come ye sinners poor and needy
Weak and wounded, sick and sore.

Beach Spring, OSH 81: 8.7

Lord I cannot let Thee go
Till a blessing Thou bestow.

Cookham, SH 8: 7.7

It is obvious that verses such as the above would normally begin on the downbeat of the music, while verses in iambic and anapaestic meters would begin on the upbeat. It is obvious too that in the basic musical setting of any line there are two choices: one can make all the note values the same for both accented and unaccented syllables, or the accented syllables can be given longer note values than the unaccented syllables. This is illustrated in two settings of the same anapaestic text in *The Original Sacred Harp*:[8]

It is natural also to fill out a short line with a longer note value or to have a longer note value at the end of a stanza or section so that the musical phrases may be the same length. A glance at any standard hymnal will show dozens of examples. A verse quoted above will illustrate the point:

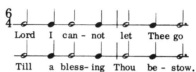

So far everything that has been said will apply to the setting of practically any hymn verse as a matter of course. However, there are certain rhythmic factors that are peculiar to the Old Harps; some of these have been already touched upon in Chapter III. The three characteristics that follow are also representative of much of the secular folk music of the southeastern part of the United States. But whether folk music has influenced the Old Harps in these respects or vice versa, the author hesitates to say. It is probably the former, though Dr. Jackson, who knew as much about the matter as anyone, is silent on these points. These characteristics are: (1) There is a strong tendency toward rather regular rhythmic structural patterns. (2) There is a preference for long note values on upbeats, particularly at the beginning of a phrase or section. (3) These folk composers and arrangers like to put two pitches on a single syllable of the text somewhere in the measure. Frequently one pitch will be non-harmonic. This device does not, of course, affect the time value allotted to that syllable.

Before these points are taken up there are two further facts that must

8. "Royal Band," OSH 360, and "South Union," OSH 344.

be considered: (1) added choruses may be in a different poetic meter than the hymn proper, and (2) many of the hymns are not barred correctly, as was noted in Chapter III. Take, for instance, the hymn "Jackson," OSH 317, in Long Meter:

I am a stranger here below
And what I am is hard to know
I am so vile, so prone to sin
I fear I am not born again.[9]

Ex. 136

Ex. 137. Jackson rebarred

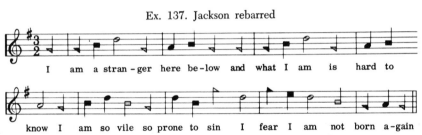

The barring of the melody in *The Original Sacred Harp* is shown in Ex. 136. It will be observed that a weak syllable comes on a strong beat in every third measure. If the tune is barred according to the verse meter and the rhythmic pattern already set up, the metric signature becomes 3/2 and the strong beats of the measures carry accented syllables of the text (Ex. 137). The last beat of each measure is an unaccented syllable on a longer note value, thus providing an interesting example of (2) above and also of rhythmic pattern no. 1 in Chapter III.

The metric irregularity in the Old Harp books is due almost entirely to the feeling that important upbeats should be on longer note values,

9. Notice that "again" rhymes with "sin"; this is an example of older English pronunciation still fairly common in the rural South. Another example occurs in "Prospect," OSH 30, where "are" rhymes with "there."

point (2) as noted above. At first glance this would appear to be at variance with point (1), but closer examination will show that the rhythmic *structure*, that is, the repetition of phrases or measures of like rhythmic pattern, is apt to be regular. The exception has already been noted: hymns which have choruses in a different meter than the verse.

Ex. 138. Separation, SH 30. Originally barred in 4/4 throughout. It is a simple alternation of duple and triple measures.

EX. 139. Liverpool, SH 1. Originally barred in 4/4 throughout. Simple alternation of rhythmic phrase patterns.

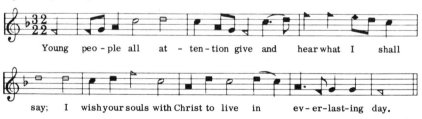

An examination of the following examples will make all this much clearer than words. In each case the hymn has been rebarred according to the metrical accent of the words (Ex. 138). Other hymns having this pattern of simple alternation of meters follow. All are either in L.M. or C.M. and all were originally barred in 4/4: Detroit, SH 40; Rockbridge, SH 288; Supplication, SH 5; and Sweet Rivers, SH 166.

There is no example of regular alternation between duple and triple measures in compound meter (Ex. 139).

Three other hymns, all in C.M. and all originally in 4/4, have the same pattern as Ex. 139. They are Land of Rest, OSH 285; Messiah, SH 97; and Minister's Farewell, SH 14.

Ex. 140. Immensity, SH 319. Originally barred in 6/4 throughout. First and last section in regular meter, middle section irregular.

The third pattern differs from the first two in that it can occur either in simple or compound time (Ex. 140). Hymns having this metric structure come in both simple and compound meters and are mostly C.M. There are six others:

1. Columbus, SH 55. Written in 6/4 throughout, it is in C.M. Its close relative "Hopewell," NH 37, is in 6/8 but has the same structure.
2. Converted Thief, OSH 44. Also in 6/4, it is in C.M.D.
3. Parting Hand, SH 113. In 6/4, it is the only member of this group other than the given example to be in L.M.
4. Pleasant Hill, SH 66. In 6/4 and C.M.
5. Salvation, SH 84. It is written in 4/4 throughout and is in C.M.
6. Tennessee, SH 28. Also in 4/4 and C.M.

The next pattern is exactly backward. It tends to be used for verses in L.M. (Ex. 141). Note that only one of the hymns in this group is in compound meter. There are only four, and they are:

1. Devotion, SH 13. In 4/4 throughout. L.M.
2. Distress, SH 22. Also in 4/4 and L.M.
3. Mission, OSH 204. In 6/8 and L.M.D.
4. New Orleans, SH 76. Again in 4/4 but in C.M.

Ex. 141. The Watchman's Call, SH 65. The first and last sections are in irregular meter; the second section is regular. The original metric signature is 4/4 throughout.

Ex. 142. The Enquirer, OSH 74. It is written in 6/4 throughout and is the only one of the three hymns in this group to be in C.M. Note that by applying the principles of modal analysis in Chapter III this tune is definitely Dorian. The section plan according to beats in measures is 2–3–2–2.

In the last of the metric patterns all sections have the same pattern of measure alteration. There are few examples of this pattern, and only two patterns of measure alteration seem to be used (Ex. 142). Two other hymns having the same general plan, though both are in L.M., are the following:

1. Days of Worship, OSH 60. Written throughout in 4/4, the section plan according to measures is 3–3–3–4. It is in L.M.D.
2. Devotion, OSH 48. The plan is exactly the same as in the above, except the meter is L.M.

As has been said above, hymns in one verse meter may have a chorus in a different meter. "Ecstasy," whose chorus has already been quoted in this chapter, is an excellent example (Ex. 143). Though the entire hymn is written in 4/4, it is obvious that the chorus would be much better in 3/2.

Ex. 143. Ecstasy, OSH 106

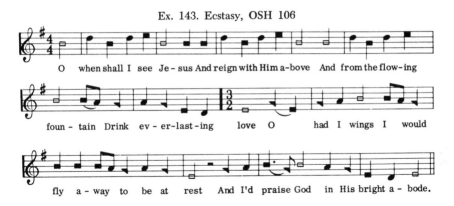

It was indicated in Chapter III that many folk hymns have some sort of misbarring; about a fourth of these are found to be perfectly regular in meter when bar lines are correctly placed, the others have mixed meters in various patterns, the most common having been shown above. Since Long and Common Meters (or either of these doubled) are used for over 52 per cent of all the folk hymns, and since these meters lend themselves to a wide variety of rhythmic treatment, most misbarrings occur in these verse meters. There are, however, examples of misbarrings in other hymn meters: "The Romish Lady" (SH 82), "Zion's Light" (SH 270), and "Bound for Canaan"(SH 193) are all in 7.6 meter. "The

Church's Desolation" (OSH 89) is the only tune in 7.8 meter to be misbarred; it is in a perfectly regular 3/2 though the printed signature is 4/4. There are two examples of misbarrings in 7.9 meter: "Weary Pilgrim" (OSH 323) and "Martial Trumpet" (SH 61).

Of the remaining hymns that are misbarred, no matter what the verse meter, most fall into some logical pattern of their own. A typical example is "Love" (OSH 303), which has the measure pattern of beats 2–3–2–2, 3–3–2–3, 2–3–2–2 (Ex. 144).

Ex. 144. Love, OSH 303

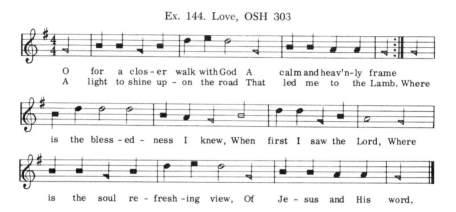

X

Even the simplest melody shows relationships of pitch (intervals), of time value (rhythm), of grouping (phrases) etc., in other words, has "form."

Apel, *Harvard Dictionary of Music*
"Form (in music)"

THE TERM "form" is used rather loosely in music to cover a great many aspects, and many books have been written on its various implications. So, before beginning a discussion of form in the folk hymns, it might be well to define the term as it will be used in this chapter. Since the aspects of shape and rhythmic patterns have already been covered, "form" in this chapter is going to be restricted to the last of the elements mentioned in the quotation above: the grouping of phrases, particularly with reference to the patterns of phrase repetition, the musical phrase coinciding with one line of the verse. Furthermore, certain ways of varying a phrase without affecting its essential character in the pattern of repetition have been recognized. These are the following: (1) by adding or subtracting notes as the lines of the verse have more or fewer syllables; (2) by ornamentation; (3) by sequence; (4) by changing the cadence from suspensive to conclusive, or, less frequently, the other way about.

The simplest structure would be a single phrase repeated over and over, with a conclusive cadence only after the final repetition. The folk hymns are slightly more complicated than this; the simplest of them are based on two musical ideas, each a phrase long, which we may represent, not very originally, as A and B. The possible combinations to form the average four-phrase tune would be the following: (1) AABB; (2) ABAB; (3) AABA; (4) ABBA; (5) AAAB; (6) ABAA; (7) ABBB.

The tune "Marietta," NH 90, would thus represent the first of these possibilities. The verse has the meter 8.8.8.6, so the last musical phrase is a few notes short (Ex. 145). Only two other tunes in the list of folk hymns have the same form. These are "Morality," SH 44, and "Still Better," OSH 166.

Ex. 145. Marietta, form AABB, rebarred

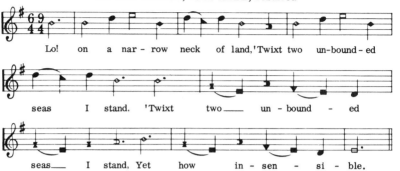

Lo!   on   a   nar - row   neck   of land,'Twixt two   un–bound - ed

seas   I   stand.   'Twixt   two____   un - bound   -   ed

seas____   I   stand, Yet   how   in - sen   -   si - ble.

Ex. 146. To Die No More, form ABAB, rebarred

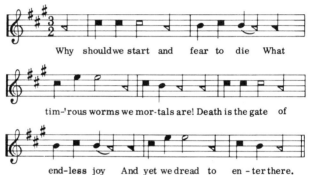

Why   should we start   and   fear   to   die   What

tim-'rous worms we mor-tals are! Death is the gate   of

end-less joy   And yet we dread to   en - ter there.

Ex. 147. Cusseta, form AABA, rebarred

Show   pit - y   Lord,   O   Lord for - give; Let   a   re -

pent - ing   reb - el   live   Are   not   Thy   mer - cies

large and free? May   not   a   sin - ner   trust in   Thee?

The form ABAB is represented by only two tunes, "Long Sought Home," OSH 235, and "To Die No More," OSH 111. The latter is quoted by way of illustration in Ex. 146.

"New Britain," SH 8, and "Cusseta," OSH 73, have the formal structure AABA. The latter is quoted in Ex. 147.

There are five examples of the form ABBA: "Ester," OSH 37, "Millenium," OSH 130, "Imandra New," SH 34, "Fellowship," OSH 330, and "Golden Hill," NH 81. This last tune illustrates the form (Ex. 148).

The verse of the tune "Ecstasy" in Ex. 143 illustrates the form AAAB. Other tunes with the same form are "Happiness," SH 40, "Marston," NH 131, and "Ninety-Third," SH 7.

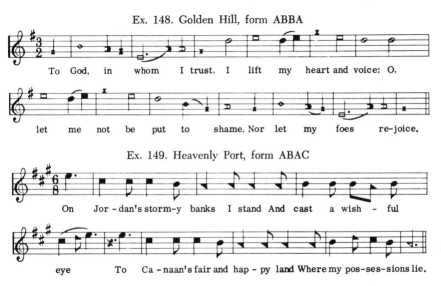

Ex. 148. Golden Hill, form ABBA

To God, in whom I trust, I lift my heart and voice: O,

let me not be put to shame, Nor let my foes re-joice.

Ex. 149. Heavenly Port, form ABAC

On Jor - dan's storm-y banks I stand And cast a wish - ful

eye To Ca - naan's fair and hap - py land Where my pos-ses-sions lie.

The last two possibilities of the two-unit melody are not found in the folk hymns.

If a third melodic unit is added, there are five possibilities of arrangement: (1) ABAC; (2) ABBC; (3) AABC; (4) ABCA; (5) ABCB. The first possibility is represented by four tunes; "Heavenly Port," OSH 378, is quoted as an example (Ex. 149). Other tunes having this form are "The Dying Californian," OSH 410, "Kambia," SH 154, and "Lone Pilgrim," SH 256.

The form ABBC, less common than some of the others, may be illustrated by "Charlestown," SH 23 (Ex. 150).

The third form can be found in "Confidence," SH 33 (Ex. 151). Other

Ex. 150. Charlestown, form **ABBC**

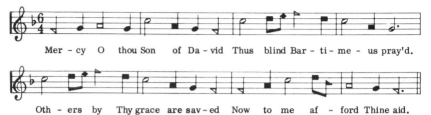

Mer - cy O thou Son of Da - vid Thus blind Bar - ti - me - us pray'd.

Oth - ers by Thy grace are sav - ed Now to me af - ford Thine aid.

Ex. 151. Confidence, form **AABC**

Though trou - bles as - sail and dan - gers af - fright Though

friends should all fail and foes all u - nite Yet

one thing se - cures us what - ev - er be - tide, The

Scrip - ture as - sures us the Lord will pro - vide.

Ex. 152. Devotion, form **ABCA**, rebarred

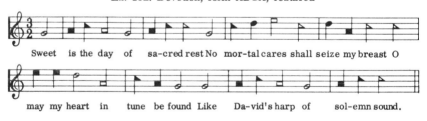

Sweet is the day of sa-cred rest No mor-tal cares shall seize my breast O

may my heart in tune be found Like Da-vid's harp of sol-emn sound.

tunes in this form are "Cleburne," OSH 314, in which the entire pattern is repeated, "Jackson," OSH 317, and "Kedron," SH 3.

The fourth form, ABCA, is represented by "Distress," SH 22, "Dunlap's Creek," SH 276, "Horton," OSH 330, "French Broad," SH 266, "Idumea," SH 31, and "Devotion," SH 13 (see Ex. 152).

In all examples of the form ABCB the last phrase is a refrain first heard as the second phrase. The tune "Anticipation," NH 75, is a good example (Ex. 153). Other examples are "Contented Soldier," SH 314, "In That Morning," SH 194, "Golden Harp," OSH 274, "Heaven's My Home," OSH 119, "Never Turn Back," OSH 378, "Done with the World," OSH 88, and "Farewell," OSH 461.

The addition of a D phrase results in a four-phrase tune that is through-composed. Such tunes, for the most part, are given unity through figure repetition; this not only occurs between the second and third phrases where we have learned to expect it, but between other

Ex. 153. Anticipation, form ABCB

phrases as well. See Ex. 154 and 155. Other tunes in this form that have typical figure repetition are "Arkansas," OSH 271, "Bishop," OSH 420, "Columbiana," OSH 56, "Concord," NH 46, "Consolation," SH 17, "Davis," SH 15, "Desire for Piety," OSH 76, "Fight On," OSH 385, "Fleeting Days," OSH 348, "Land of Rest," OSH 285, "Liverpool," SH 1, and "New Year," NH 67.

Through-composed tunes of four phrases with no particular figure repetition are "Condescension," SH 312, "Corinth," OSH 32, "Detroit," OSH 39, and "Dying Minister," OSH 38.

It has already been noted that one AABC form was repeated within a single eight-line verse.[1] The ABCD pattern is also occasionally repeated. "Deep Spring," NH 93, "Hebrew Children," OSH 133, and "Heavenly March," SH 253, are examples of this enlarged form. In the first of these the extra words are simply a repetition of the original

1. "Cleburne," OSH 314, noted as an example of Form AABC in this chapter.

Ex. 154. Odem, OSH 295, form ABCD with figure repetition

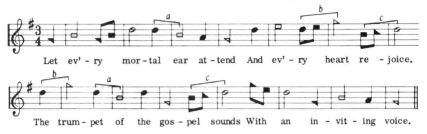

Let ev' - ry mor - tal ear at - tend And ev' - ry heart re - joice.

The trum - pet of the gos - pel sounds With an in - vit - ing voice.

Ex. 155. Ogletree, OSH 138, same form

Fre - quent the day of God re - turns To shed its quick' - ning

beams And yet how slow de - vo - tion burns How lang - uid are its flames.

Ex. 156. Holy Manna, OSH 59, SH 103, NH 107

Breth - ren we have met to wor - ship And a -
Will you pray with all your pow - er While we

dore the Lord our God
try to preach the Word? All is vain un - less the Spi - rit

Of the Ho - ly One comes down Breth - ren pray and

ho - ly man - na Will be show - ered all a - round.

verse; "Hebrew Children" has an eight-line verse, while in "Heavenly March" the ABCD melody is heard three times—an extra verse is added and then the words of this are repeated.

About 10 per cent of the tunes fall into regular three-part forms, six phrases with the last two like the first. Most of these use four melodic elements in the arrangement AB CD AB. A few tunes use only three elements; "Newman," OSH 321, has the pattern AB CC AB. "Holy Manna," which is included in all three books and is one of the most popular of all the tunes, is rare in that it uses only two elements in the pattern AA BB AA (Ex. 156).

Ex. 157. Happy Land. The last section is made up of one phrase from Section I and one phrase from Section II.

Another typical practice in six-phrase tunes (or eight-phrase, if the first two phrases are repeated) is to form either the middle or the last section by using one new phrase and one repeated phrase or by using two phrases from different sections. "Happy Land," OSH 354, is a good example (Ex. 157). Parenthetically, this is the tune used for the popular "Old Soldiers Never Die" during the Second World War. Other similar tunes are "All is Well," SH 306, "An Address for All," SH 99, "Antioch," OSH 277, "The Church's Desolation," OSH 89, and "Hopewell," NH 37.

Tunes with five phrases (or seven, if the first two are repeated) are characterized by repetition of the words of the fourth (or sixth) phrase. These frequently have the basic pattern ABCD, plus an added phrase of new material, as in Ex. 158. Other tunes of the same type are "Albion," NH 12, "Fairfield," SH 48, "Funeral Thought," SH 257, and "Isles of the South," SH 86.

Tunes larger than five phrases always have some phrase repetition; this has already been shown in six-phrase tunes, and the fact is equally true of tunes having a greater number of phrases. There are only about

5 per cent of these latter, and the repetition patterns vary a great deal.

One further peculiarity of folk hymns should be mentioned. Sixteen of them have ornamental phrase extensions, usually at the end of the penultimate section, as in Ex. 159.

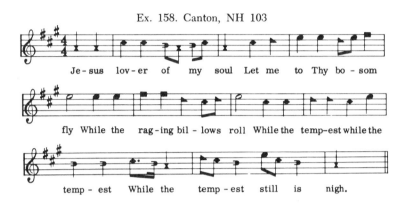

Ex. 158. Canton, NH 103

Je-sus lov-er of my soul Let me to Thy bo - som fly While the rag-ing bil - lows roll While the temp-est while the temp - est While the temp - est still is nigh.

Ex. 159. Christian Contemplation, NH 48

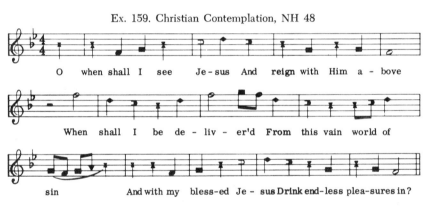

O when shall I see Je-sus And reign with Him a - bove When shall I be de - liv - er'd From this vain world of sin And with my bless-ed Je - sus Drink end-less plea-sures in?

There is little correlation between these formal patterns and those of rhythmic structure noted in the preceding chapter. Rhythmic pattern 2, a simple alternation of phrase rhythmic patterns, included only two four-phrase examples, both of which have the formal pattern ABCD. Of course it is obvious that if a tune has the formal structure AABA, for example, the rhythmic structure for the A phrases is going to be the same, but if the rhythmic pattern of two phrases is the same it is by no means always true that the melodic line will be the same. It may be safely said that repetition of rhythmic patterns has little to do with the form of a tune.

XI

What's in a name?

Shakespeare, *Romeo and Juliet*
Act II, scene 2

THE NAMES of the anthems, fuguing pieces, psalm tunes, hymn tunes, and folk hymns in the Old Harp books offer a fascinating study of their own, and one that can be undertaken with no particular thought of scholarly significance. Such a study is tremendously interesting. It is also maddening.

Some names are perfectly obvious, some give a hint of the part of the country in which they originated; some have a sort of hidden significance; and some seem to have no meaning at all. Some tunes always have the same name, some usually do, and some, particularly the folk hymns, seem to take a new name each time they appear in a new book.

As a general rule of thumb, the Early American pieces go by the same name in every book. The compositions given in Chapter II are apt to appear under these names in almost any book. There are a few exceptions: "Liberty" (no. 29) is called "Prosperity" in *The Musical Instructor* but in none of the other six books in which it was found. "Ninety-fifth" is called "Refuge" in *The Timbrel of Zion* but in none of the other books in which it appeared. It is true that "Ninety-third" appears under a variety of aliases, but, as was mentioned in Chapter III, this may well be an early folk hymn. Jackson lists it as such, and it has many folk hymn characteristics; in fact, it has been treated as a folk hymn in previous chapters. However, it is always wise to check when one finds a seemingly constant name. The "Concord" of OSH 313 is by no means the "Concord" of NH 46 and SH 321, nor is "Middletown" always the same as "Middleton." Sometimes it is and sometimes it isn't, for the folk hymn usually sung to the words of "Amazing Grace" is also called "Middleton."

Some of the names of these early tunes recall incidents associated with the first Great Awakening. "Enfield," for instance, is the name of the town where, in 1741, Jonathan Edwards delivered the sermon "by

which, if he be remembered at all, he is likely to be known forever."[1]
"Windham" takes its name from the town in Connecticut where the
Reverend Thomas Clap accused young Robert Breck of heresy. Breck's
trial in 1735 was one of the reasons that the first stage of the Great
Awakening ended so quickly; Edwards was associated with this trial,
and "it was the first act in the drama of his dismissal."[2]

Other New England place names found among the Early American
tune names are these:

1. Bridgewater: in Litchfield County, Connecticut
2. Claremont: in Sullivan County, New Hampshire
3. Concord: in Middlesex County, Massachusetts
4. Greenfield: either in Franklin County, Massachusetts, or Hills-
boro County, New Hampshire
5. Greenwich: in Fairfield County, Connecticut
6. Middletown: in Middlesex County, Connecticut. There is a
"Middleton" in Massachusetts and another in New Hampshire.
7. Milford is a common New England place name, occurring in
Connecticut, Delaware, Maine, Massachusetts, New Hampshire,
and New Jersey.
8. Montgomery: could be either in Hampden County, Massachusetts, or in Franklin County, Virginia. The tune might equally well
be named for the Revolutionary hero.
9. Stafford: in Tolland County, Connecticut
10. Suffield: this might be the town in Connecticut or the county
in Massachusetts.
11. Sutton is a town both in New Hampshire and in Vermont.
12. Yarmouth: could be either in Barnstable County, Massachusetts, or in Cumberland County, Maine.

"Northfield" is also a place name, and it has a well-known and
amusing story connected with it. Ingalls was, of course, a singing school
master, and in the course of the travels connected with his profession
stopped at the tavern in Northfield and ordered dinner. It was slow in
coming, "but the inevitable 'how long?' that formulated itself in his
hungry thoughts, instead of sharpening into profane complaint, fell into
the rhythm of Watts' sacred line."[3] The line in question is "How long,
dear Saviour, O how long, Shall this bright hour delay?"

1. Perry Miller, *Jonathan Edwards*, p. 145.
2. Henry Bamford Parkes, *Jonathan Edwards*, Chapter VIII.
3. Butterfield-Brown, p. 508.

Many others of these tunes derive their names directly from the words with which they are associated. "Easter Anthem," "Farewell Anthem," "Funeral Anthem," and "David's Lamentation" are, of course, obvious. Less obvious are the following:

1. Coronation: from the refrain "And crown Him, Lord of all."
2. Creation: from "Let every creature join / To praise th'eternal God."
3. Exhortation: from "Now in the heat of youthful blood / Remember your Creator, God."
4. Heavenly Vision: the text is taken from Revelation.
5. Invitation: from the words of the fuguing part "Come my beloved, haste away, / Cut short the hours of thy delay."
6. Jubilee: from Cowper's text "Hark the Jubilee is sounding."
7. Liberty: from the verse "No more beneath th'opressive hand / Of tyranny we groan."
8. Majesty: suggested by the words "On cherubs and on cherubim / Full royally He rode."
9. New Jerusalem: from the words of the second stanza "The New Jerusalem comes down / Adorned with shining grace."
10. Ocean: from "Thy works of glory, Mighty Lord, / That rul'st the boist'rous seas."
11. Spring: from "The scattered clouds are fled at last, / The rain is gone, the winter's past."

The folk hymns take their names in much the same way, with perhaps a bit more variety. In general we may distinguish the following sources of the names: (1) from places; (2) from the Bible; (3) people; (4) the secular ballad from which the tune was taken; and (5) derived directly or indirectly from the words.

Place names may be of many kinds: countries, states, counties, towns, country churches, rivers, and so on. By far the largest number of tunes are named for towns; this is not surprising, since the southern singing school masters traveled a lot, and it was good business to name a song after a town where a successful school had been held. Here is a list of tunes probably deriving their names from towns or counties:

1. Albany: it is unlikely that this was named for the city in New York. It was "written" by M. L. Swan, the compiler of *The Harp* (and *The New Harp*) *of Columbia* who worked in the South. There is an Albany in Dougherty County, Georgia, and another in Clinton County, Kentucky.

2. Antioch: by F. C. Wood, a Georgian. This may have been named for the Biblical city, but more probably it derives its name from the town in Davidson County, Tennessee.

3. Bellvue: there is a town of this name in Campbell County, Kentucky.

4. Bishop: either the town in Colbert County, Alabama, or the one in Oconee County, Georgia.

5. Canton: there are towns by this name in Georgia, Kentucky, and North Carolina.

6. Charlton: this seems to take its name from the county of the same name in Georgia. It is by L. P. Breedlove, who lived in the mid-nineteenth century and worked largely in Georgia.

7. Cleburne: this is undoubtedly named for Cleburne County, Georgia. It is attributed to S. M. Denson.

8. Columbiana: attributed to D. P. White, this can only be named for Columbiana in Shelby County, Alabama.

9. Columbus: there are towns named Columbus in Georgia and Mississippi. There is also a Columbus County in North Carolina.

10. Corinth: this could have been named for the Biblical city, though there are towns of this name in Kentucky and West Virginia.

11. Cusseta: improbably there are two towns having this odd name. One is in Chambers County, Alabama, the other in Chattahoochee County, Georgia.

12. Detroit: this of course could be the Michigan city, but is probably the town of the same name in Lamar County, Alabama.

13. Dudley: there are towns of this name in both Georgia and North Carolina.

14. Edgefield: probably Edgefield, South Carolina.

15. Florence: this could be named for a female friend, though there are towns of this name in Kentucky, Mississippi, South Carolina, and Tennessee. In the North the name is found in Massachusetts, New Jersey, and Vermont.

16. Fairfield: is undoubtedly named for Fairfield, Connecticut, since this is one of the older hymns and is of northern origin.

17. Golden Hill: there is apparently only one Golden Hill in America, in Dorchester County, Maryland. This tune is sometimes attributed to Chapin; if this attribution is correct the tune may commemorate a pause in the elder Chapin's southward trek after the Revolution.

18. Greensborough or Greensboro is such a common name that it is impossible to guess which town is thus commemorated. Likely

candidates are in Alabama, Georgia, North Carolina, Pennsylvania, and Vermont.

19. Hopewell: since this tune is attributed to William Caldwell (of Maryville, Tennessee), the Hopewell meant is likely that in Cleburne County, Georgia.

20. Horton: in Marshall County, Alabama.

21. Lancaster: attributed to "Swan" in *The New Harp of Columbia.* This would be M. L. and not Timothy; the reference is probably to Lancaster in Smith County, Tennessee.

22. Liverpool: according to *The Original Sacred Harp* this first appeared in *Mercer's Cluster,* which was compiled by the Reverend Jesse Mercer of Powellton, Georgia. If so, the name may refer not to the English city, but to the town in Macon County, Georgia.

23. Marietta: attributed to "Swan" (M. L) in *The New Harp of Columbia,* the Marietta referred to is probably the town just over the Tennessee line in Cobb County, Georgia.

24. Marston: in Richmond County, North Carolina.

25. Monroe: this may have been named for the president or for one of the towns of the same name in Georgia, Kentucky, or Tennessee, or for Monroe County in Alabama.

26. New Britain: there is only one town of this name in the United States; it is in Hartford County, Connecticut.

27. New Harmony: can this be the Utopian community in Indiana?

28. Primrose: perhaps for the flower, though there is a town of this name in Providence County, Rhode Island.

29. Prospect: there are many towns of this name. The most likely are in Connecticut, Kentucky, Ohio, Pennsylvania, and Tennessee.

30. Rockbridge is a county in Virginia.

31. Rockingham: a town in Georgia, North Carolina, or Vermont, and a county in New Hampshire, North Carolina, or Virginia.

32. Temple: probably the town in Carroll County, Georgia.

33. Vernon: there is a town of this name in Lamar County, Georgia.

34. Victoria: since this is attributed to the Breedlove who assisted in the revision of *The Sacred Harp* of 1850, the tune probably takes its name from the town in Coffee County, Alabama.

35. Warrenton: there are towns of this name in Georgia, North Carolina, and Virginia.

36. Webster: there is a Webster County in Georgia, Kentucky, Mississippi, and West Virginia.

States lending their names to folk hymns include Tennessee, Louisiana, and Rhode Island; foreign countries are represented by Cuba,

Egypt, and Sardinia. Names of rivers are seldom used: French Broad, in *The Southern Harmony,* is one of the few. (A ribald northern friend laughed his head off at this one.) Spring Place is the name of a country church; New Bethany, New Bethel, and Dunlap's Creek are probably also church names.

Biblical names, besides the Antioch and Corinth already mentioned, include the following:

1. Idumea: mentioned in Is. 34:5, Ezekiel 35:15, and Mark 3:8.
2. Jordan and Jordan's Shore: the river in which Jesus was baptized.
3. Kedron and Sweet Gliding Kedron: the brook mentioned, among other places, in 2 Sam. 15:23 and John 18:1.
4. Messiah: Daniel 9:25, John 1:41, etc.
5. Salem: Gen. 14:18, Heb. 7:1.

Some tunes are named for people; perhaps for the person who composed or arranged the tune, perhaps for the person who wrote the words. Only occasionally is a tune named in honor of another person. Besides the possibilities mentioned in the first list in this chapter, the following tunes are named for people:

1. Bruce's Address: the tune of "Scots what hae wi' Wallace Bled" is, of course, named for Robert the Bruce.
2. Davis: possibly for R. H. Davis who, the OSH says (p. 119), "was prominent in the sacred musical conventions and societies from 1859 up to the early seventies."
3. Odem: for L. P. Odem, instrumental in the 1936 revision of *The Original Sacred Harp.*
4. Rees: for J. P. Rees (or Reese) who was born in Georgia in 1828 and died in 1900. He was well known as a leader and as president both of the Southern Musical Convention and the Chattahoochee Singing Convention.
5. Ragan: for Reverend R. G. Ragan of Davisville, Alabama, original "composer" of the music.
6. Sawyer's Exit: for the Reverend S. B. Sawyer, author of the words, which were said to be composed on the day of his death.
7. White: the OSH says this was composed by Elder Edmund Dumas in 1856, in honor of B. F. White, compiler of *The Sacred Harp.*

The above, it must be emphasized, are only the names about which the author has been able to get definite information or about which one can be relatively sure. Such names as "Willoughby" and "Kelley" are pretty sure to have belonged to actual people, but there is no indication who these people were.

A few tunes take their names, directly or indirectly, from the secular folk songs from which they were adapted. There are three of them:

1. Captain Kidd: to be found under this name in *Our Familiar Songs and Who Made Them,* with secular words.[4]
2. France: this name is derived only indirectly. Jackson gives a reference in AnS 329 to Bayard, *Hill Country Tunes,* No. 90.[5] The tune in question is mentioned by the author as being related to "France" in NH. One of its names is "Napoleon Crossing the Rhine."
3. Romish Lady: this is a more or less straightforward version of the English ballad of the same name.

Tunes deriving their names from the words are so many that a complete list would take up far too much space. In general they may be classified under three headings:

1. Titles derived from the subject matter: The Converted Thief, The Dying Californian, etc.
2. Titles quoting words used: Highlands of Heaven (Sinner, will you go To the highlands of Heaven?); In that Morning (Jesus my all to heaven is gone / And we'll all shout together in that morning).
3. Titles whose sense is derived from the words but the words are not actually a part of the title: Sweet Prospect (On Jordan's stormy banks I stand and cast a wishful eye / To Canaan's fair and happy land, etc.); Desire for Piety ('Tis my desire with God to walk), etc.

These exercises are all good fun, and it takes very little trouble to run down the information, though it means little except the satisfaction of an incurable curiosity. More meaningful, more interesting, and decidedly more exasperating is the search for a given folk hymn tune through the index of some old manual, since the same tune may go under half a dozen different names. The discipline is meaningful since (1) obviously, the earlier the book in which it is found, the earlier the tune, and (2) the variants of the tune have a musicological interest.

4. See footnote 16 in Chapter IV.
5. Samuel Preston Bayard, *Hill Country Tunes: Instrumental Folk Music of Southwestern Pennsylvania* (Philadelphia, 1944).

The obvious first step in running down a tune is to look at the index of the book one is examining and to note the names with which one is familiar. Fortunately, many tune titles remain fairly constant; we have already seen that this is apt to be the case with the Early American pieces, and it is also apt to be true of the older folk hymns. Next, one must compare these familiarly named tunes with the ones already known. Sometimes they are the same, sometimes not.

Sometimes a name in the index may give no more than a clue; it takes no great intelligence to suppose that a tune listed as "Social Band" in *The Southern Harmony* might just conceivably be the same as "Clamanda" in *The Original Sacred Harp*, the words of which begin "Come all ye lovely social band." Another example of this sort of thing is the tune called "Happy Matches" in *The Original Sacred Harp. The Beauties of Harmony* has a tune called "Few Happy Matches" which proves to be identical, even as to key. But on the other hand, who would suspect that this tune is the same as "Willoughby" in *The Southern Harmony* or in *The Methodist Collection of Hymns and Tunes* of 1849?

And so the next step in this tune detection is to read through every tune in each manual, hoping that one's memory for several hundred tunes is good enough to spot the ones that sound familiar. Actually, this is not such a job as it sounds. If one has attended many Old Harp singings in the course of a couple of decades, it is not too hard to give the Old Harp name to a familiar tune.

The following list includes, with a few exceptions, only tunes listed in Appendix I, and notes whether Dr. Jackson gives any of the alternative titles. A key to the abbreviations used is appended at the end of this chapter.

1. Anticipation: NH 75. Jackson in DE 238 calls it "Part No More."
2. Antioch: OSH 277. Jackson in SF 166 says it is also called "Shout On" and "Pray On."
3. Babe of Bethlehem: SH 78. Variants are called "Milton" in KnH and "Staunton" in SKyH. Jackson does not mention the alternatives.
4. Beach Spring: OSH 81. This is called "Fount of Glory" in SH. Jackson gives the same tune, but in a different rhythm, in SF 56 as "Missionary Farewell."
5. Bellvue: OSH 72. This is called "Christian's Farewell" in SH, "Protection" in NH, UHC, KnH, and GChM. It is called "Huger" in SacMel and "Foundation" in modern hymnals. DE 145 lists this tune as "How Firm a Foundation."

6. Bozrah: SH 39. This is called "The Traveller" in OSH, "Messiah" in CrH. Jackson in SF 138 notes the resemblance to "New Orleans," SH 76.

7. Bruce's Address: SH 132, NH 109. This is called "Wallace" in ChH and GChM, "Overton" in TZ, "Caledonia" in AmVoc, and "Friends of Freedom Swell the Song" in SacMel. Jackson in SF 112 calls it "Friends of Freedom."

8. Canton: NH 103, UHC. This is called "Interrogation" in SH and "Hark my Soul" in CrH. SF 64 lists it under the latter title.

9. Captain Kidd, SH 50, MoH, is called "Green Meadow" (Green Meddow, Green Meadows) in SKyH, KnH, and AuH. It is called "How Precious is the Name" in AmVoc. SF 142 does not mention other names.

10. Carnsville, OSH 109, is called "The Christian" in SH 26.

11. Charlestown (Charleston): SH 23, OSH 52. This name is also used in GChM and KnH. It is called "Bartimeus" in PrPs, MeHT, SL, CrMin, and WChH (gives both names). It is called "David" in BapHT. In the Funk *Choral Music* of 1816 it is called "Seelen Weide, meine Freude," and, in a different meter, it is called "Swaine" in Phil. In AmVoc it appears as "Deal Gently with Thy Servants, Lord." DE 80 does not list the other titles.

12. Cheerful: SH 91. AnS 259 lists this as "O How I Have Longed."

13. Christian Contemplation: NH 48. The same name is used in KnH; it is called "Faithful Soldier" in SH 122 and in WChH. It is listed as "Sweet Prospect" in UHC. SF 59 lists only "Faithful Soldier."

14. Christian Soldier: SH 45, OSH 57. It is also called this in WestPs and WChH. In NH 112 the same tune is called "Humility." WChH also has a variant (in a different meter) called "Volunteers." SF 68 lists no other title.

15. Christian Song: SH 129, OSH 240, NH 185. It is to be found under this title in MoH, SacMel, and UHC. It is called "The Tedious Hour" in ICH. AnS 169 lists the latter title.

16. Church's Desolation: OSH 89. It is also called this in SacMel, WestPs, WChH, and Phil. WChH also gives the title "Mourner's Lamentation." Similar tunes are to be found in ICH called "Mourning Souls" and in Rev under the title "Hallowed Spot." "Overton" in SKyH has some similarities. SF 28, though it gives the Ingalls reference, does not list the alternative name.

17. Clamanda (Clamandra): OSH 42. It also appears under this name in SKyH, UHC, KnH, AUH, and ChH. The tune is called "Social Band" in SH and "Ardella" in TZ. In WestPs it is listed as "Amboy." SF 93 does not list the appearances in SH or TZ though

Jackson used these books, nor do the other titles appear. Variants appear in ICH ("Shouting Hymn") and AmVoc and Rev ("Far from my Thoughts").

18. Columbus: SH 55. It appears under this title in WChH and as "Hopewell" in NH, UHC, and KnH. SF 75 lists the tune as "Columbus" with no mention of the alternative title.

19. Concord: SH 321, NH 46. It is called by this name in KnH, UHC, and WChH. It appears as "Dying Christian" in OSH. DE 161 gives only the UHC reference.

20. Condescension: SH 312. It is listed under this name in MoH, KnH, SacMel, WestPs, and Phil. It is called "Adoration" in WyRepII, "Nelson" in ChrCho, and "Return" in Rev. A variant called "Judgment Day" is also in Rev. SF 30 makes no mention of other names.

21. Confidence: SH 33. It is also called by this name in LCL, Har, and MeHT. It is called "Parting" in Rev and "Nettleton" in ZH. DE 142 gives no other titles.

22. Consolation: SH 17. It is called by this name in GChM, MoH, AUH, WyRepII, UHC, WChH, and ChH. It is called "Infancy" in ChrCho. This tune is closely related to the old psalm tune "Brunswick," found, among other places, in Lyons' *Urania*. A tune closely related both to "Consolation" and to "Brunswick" is "Hiding Place," to be found in AnHR, HS, Jub, PrPs, and PsHSS. The same tune is called "Atonement" in AmVoc. DE 135 notes the resemblance to "Hiding Place."

23. Consolation New: SH 58. This is simply called "Consolation" in WyRepII, SKyH, UHC, and AUH.

24. Cookham: SH 8, OSH 81. It is to be found under this name in VH, SZ, GChM, EvM, ChH, Harm, KnH, ChH, TZ, CrMin, and WChH. It is called "True Riches" in SKyH and AUH, "Ebenezer" in WestPs, "Redeeming Love" in SoHTB, "Grace" in Phil, and "The Pearl" in BapHT. Jackson does not list this tune.

25. Crucifixion: SH 25. It also goes by this title in SKyH, AUH, KnH, AmVoc, WChH, and Phil. It is called "Atonement" in LCL, "Saw Ye my Saviour" in ChH, and "Edellium" in BapHT. SF 16 gives the tune under the name of "Saw Ye my Saviour" and the only reference as ChH.

26. Davis: SH 15. It is listed under this name in WyRepII, MoH, ChH, CrH, SacMel, and WChH. It is called "Bethel" in LCL, "New Salem" in UHC and WestPs, "The Voice of my Beloved" in AmVoc, "Beloved of Zion" in LZ, and "Beloved" in Vic, Rev, and Phil. It is called "Dulcimer" in SZ and MeHy. SF 163 mentions "Dulcimer" and "Beloved."

27. Deep Spring: NH 93. It is to be found under this name in

KnH and UHC. It is called "Longing for Home" in ChHarp and ChH, "Land of Rest" in LZ and Rev, and "Wolfe" in ChrCho. SF 35 gives only the alternative title of "Converted Thief" which was not found by the author.

28. Devotion: SH 13, OSH 48. It will be found under this name in SKyH, AUH, GChM, ChH, UHC, LZ, MoH, SacMel, WestPs, WChH, and Phil. It is called "The Penitent" in PrPs, HS, and SoHTB. SF 120 gives "Devotion" and "The Penitent."

29. Dunlap's Creek: SH 276. This tune usually keeps its name: "Dunlap's Creek" was used in nineteen of the twenty-one books in which it was found. The two exceptions were "Funeral" in SZ and "Dunlap" in Jub. SF 75 gives only "Dunlap's Creek."

30. Ecstasy, OSH 106. Jackson in SF 197 gives "Had I Wings" as the alternative title. This does not appear in either of my two editions, nor have I found the title elsewhere.

31. Elysian: SH 100, OSH 139. This is called "Harrisonburg" in SKyH and AUH; it is called "Beulah" in CHT, SZ, SSBC, BHT, PsHSS, HSP, SSS, BapHy, and HMeEC. It is called "Greenwood" in MeHT and MeHTC, and "Ives" in DevHT, SL, SoHTB, WChH, Rev, BapHT, and JasG. DE 78 lists no other titles.

32. Exhilaration: SH 54, OSH 170. SF lists as other titles "Then My Troubles Will be Over" and "I Never Shall Forget the Day" without saying where these may be found.

33. Expression: AnS 225 calls this tune "Jesus my Saviour." It is found in OSH 125.

34. Family Circle: OSH 333. DE 219 gives the alternative title as "We'll Join Heart and Hand."

35. Fiducia, SH 92. This is another of the older folk hymns and is usually found under this name; in thirteen of the books examined it was called "Fiducia." However, in UHC it is called "Sharon," and in AmVoc and Rev it is called "Amazing Grace." It goes by the name of "Heavenly Love" in LCL, and a variant in Rev is called "Bristol." DE 183 calls it "Fiducia."

36. Florence: OSH 121. It is called "Redeeming Love" in UHC, KnH, and WChH. SF 82 does not list the appearance of the tune in KnH nor the alternative title.

37. France: NH 148. This is called "Star of Bethlehem" in CrH. AnS 329 does not give this reference.

38. Garden Hymn: SH 90. It goes by this title in LCL, AmVoc, LZ, HS, DevHT, and Rev. It is called "Love Divine" in ICH, "Springhill" in WyRepII, "Bexley" in TZ, and "Garden" in SSPW and BapHy. It is called "Baltimore" in SKyH. DE 58, and a variant called "Ceylon" in SF 132, list "Baltimore" as a related tune.

39. Greenfield(s): SH 71, OSH 127, NH 16. This one is so common that it would take a page to give all the references. Look for it also under the titles "DeFleury," "Contrast," and "Newton." Even Jackson, in SF 60, simply says "etc." after giving a few references. He does not mention any other names.

40. Grieved Soul: OSH 448. This is called "Mercy" in ChH and "Boundless Mercy" in Phil; it is called "Come my Brethren" in AmVoc and Rev and "The Believer and his Soul" in WChH. DE 71 calls it "Boundless Mercy."

41. Happy Matches: OSH 96 and SH 277. It keeps this name in MeHTC, HSP, and PsHSS. It is called "Few Happy Matches" in BH and KnH; it is called "Willowby" in CHMeCh, LCL, SKyH, MeH, CrH, Harm, CrMin, and WestPs, and "Willoughby" in MeHT, SSS, BapHy, and LZ. In AnS 137 no other titles are mentioned.

42. Heavenly March, SH 253. The same tune is called "Cleburne" in OSH and "Pilgrim's Band" in HesH. Jackson lists it in AnS 91 under the latter title.

43. Highlands of Heaven: OSH 175. This is called "Sinner's Invitation" in Rev 155. SF 80 lists it under the latter title.

44. Holy Manna: SH 103, OSH 59, NH 107. It is also called by this name in KnH, TZ, and Phil. It is called "Camden" in SacMel, "Confidence" in WestPs, and "Bellenden" in SoHTB and SSPW. Rev has two variants of the tune called "Jesus Calls You" and "Gospel Power." SF 114 gives no other names.

45. Imandra (Imandria): SH 134. It is to be found under this title in SKyH, AUH, CrH, UHC, MoH, ChH, and SacMel. In Rev it is called "How Firm a Foundation." DE 126 gives only the first title.

46. Indian's Farewell: SH 25, NH 134. It is also called "Parting Friends" in SacMel, LCL, and CrH, and "Nebraska" in ChrCho. AnS 332 gives the tune under the title "When Shall we all Meet Again."

47. In That Morning: SH 194 is the same as "Sweet Morning" in OSH. SF 168 lists it as "Sweet Morning."

48. Jefferson: SH 42, OSH 148. It appears under this name in MoH, AUH, WestPs, and SocH. It is called "Pattonsburg" in UHC and is listed under this name in AnS 297.

49. Jordan's Shore: SH 318, OSH 50. In Rev it is called "On the Other Side." It is listed under the first title in DE 241.

50. Joyful: NH 141. This is called "Coburn" in Rev. SF 227, besides the first name, gives also "O That Will Be Joyful" and "Parting Hymn."

51. Kedron: SH 3, OSH 48, NH 45. It goes by this name in WyRepII,

GChM, CrH, and Phil. It is called "Garland" in AUH and "Acco-mack" in LCL, WL, EvM, ChH, and SacMel. It is related to a tune called "Hopkinton" in Belknap's *Evangelical Harmony* of 1800, and SF 57 gives a list of other related tunes but does not mention the other titles for "Kedron."

52. King of Peace: SH 6, OSH 74. It also goes by this name in KnH and WChH, but is called "Bethesda" in UHC, "Valley" in ChH, "Lovest Thou Me" in SacMel, LZ, and Rev, "Voice of Mercy" in AmVoc, "LaGrange" in WestPs, "Wallace" in ChrCho, and "Hya-cinth" in BapHT. It is listed in DE 192 as "Children of the Heavenly King."

53. Kingwood: SH 98. The same tune is called "Indian Convert" in SH 133 and "Nashville" in OSH 64. The first of these names is used in SKyH, AUH, GChM, UHC, SacMel, SocH, and BHT. "Indian Convert" is used in WChH and "Nashville" in WestPs. The tune is called "Reflection" in LCL, "Bonnell" in ChH, and "The Pilgrim's Happy Lot" in Rev. Some of these are given in DE 152.

54. Land of Rest: OSH 285. This is called "Believer" in Rev. AnS 276 makes no comment whatsoever on this tune.

55. Leander: SH 128, OSH 71, NH 61. It is listed under this name in UHC, MoH, KnH, SacMel, CrMin, WestPs, TZ, and WChH. It is called "Humility" in ICH, "Hillsborough" in SKyH, and "Land of Rest" in Phil. SF 107 gives no other titles.

56. Liverpool: SH 1, OSH 37, NH 113. It is known by this name in UCH, KnH, and WChH. It is called "Augusta" in GChM and "Jerome" in Phil. SF 7 gives the alternative title of "Solemn Ad-dress to Young People."

57. Lone Pilgrim: SH 256, OSH 341, NH 49. See also Commuck, *Indian Melodies*, 104 (1845). It is called "Missionary" in MeHT and "Pilgrim's Repose" in SacMel. It is to be found under the original name in WChH and SocH. SF 18 gives no other titles.

58. Louisiana: SH 62, OSH 207. It will be found under this title in KnH and WChH. The same melody but written in compound instead of simple meter is found in UHC as "Zion's Call." DE 140 gives two related tunes.

59. Lover of the Lord: OSH 124. This is called "You Must be a Lover of the Lord" in Rev. DE 245 gives no other titles.

60. Marietta: NH 90. This is called "Sweet Heaven" in OSH. DE 116 gives no other title.

61. Meditation: SH 4. This seems to be a very old tune with many variants. The closest are "Bourbon" in BH, SKyH, and Phil, "Dis-mission" in UHC, "Lord's Supper" in WChH (which also has "Meditation" on another page), "Peace" in Rev, and two versions

in AmVoc, "Brethren Pray" and "John Colby's Hymn." See SF 109 for "Bourbon."

62. Messiah: SH 97, OSH 131. It is to be found under this title in SKyH, AUH, and WChH. In Rev it is called "Usher." DE 105 gives no other title.

63. Middleton: NH 69. This is another very popular tune and is to be found in nearly every book. It goes under a wide variety of names; in SH it is called "New Britain," and is to be found in SF 135 under this title. Jackson gives a wide variety of titles: Harmony Grove, Symphony, Solon, and Redemption. In addition to these the author has found it as "Gallaher," KnH, and "Frugality," UHC.

64. Middlebury: SH 17. SKyH calls it "Middleberry," but WChH, SocH, and AUH stick to the more orthodox spelling. It is called "Happiness" in BapHy and HS and "Rapture" in AmVoc. Jackson does not list this tune.

65. Mission: SH 96, OSH 204. DE 15 lists it as "Young People All."

66. Morality: SH 44, NH 89. It is also to be found under this title in SKyH, MoH, AUH, SacMel, UHC, and WChH. In AmVoc it is called "Martyr's Death Song." DE 138 says it comes from a Cherokee Indian death song published in Edinburgh in 1811. The AmVoc title seems to be derived from this.

67. Mouldering Vine: SH 87. It is found under this title in SKyH, AUH, and WChH. "Sons of Sorrow," OSH 332, is the same tune with some elaboration. The tune is called "Autumn" in ChH and "Gloom of Autumn" in AmVoc. SF 22 gives "Sons of Sorrow" as an alternative title. DE 104, "Humiliation," is a variant.

68. Mullins: OSH 323. This tune is nearly always known as "Nettleton" and is associated with the words "Come Thou Fount of Every Blessing." It is called "Hallelujah" in MoH. SF 101 lists it as "Nettleton, or Sinner's Call."

69. New Hosanna: OSH 412. This is simply called "Hosanna" in SacMel, WChH, and BapHy. This tune does not appear in the Jackson books. I have included it since I have heard the tune used for a secular song called "The Farmer's Boy."

70. Ninety-third: SH 7, OSH 31, NH 25. This is another very popular tune and it is to be found in most books. It is frequently known as "Kentucky" and will be found under this title in HS, LZ, PrPs, SZ, and many others. It is called "Iowa" in SL and PsHSS, "Zuar" in TZ and CrMin, and "Delay" in ICH. DE 146 does not mention other names.

71. Old Ship of Zion: OSH 79. "There's a Better Day Coming" in WestPs is a slightly more elaborate version of the tune. SF 191 relates it to "Sweet Canaan," OSH 87 and SH 190.

72. Olney: SH 64, OSH 135. Under this title it is to be found in SKyH, UHC, KnH, GChM, MoH, AUH, SacMel, and WChH. It is called "Sigourney" in BapHT and SocH. DE 70 gives no other titles.

73. Paradise: NH 68. In DE 276 this is called "I Have a Home."

74. Pastoral Elegy: SH 147. It is called by this name in SKyH, MoH, KnH, AUH, WestPs, SacMel, and WyRepI. It is called "Corydon' in LCL, AmVoc, and Rev. DE 26 lists it under the title "Joseph and His Brethren."

75. Parting Hand: SH 113, OSH 62, NH 95. It is found under this name in WChH, SocH, and SacMel. It is called "Fillmore" in MeHy and "And Can it Be" in Rev and PsHSS. There is a closely related tune called "Tranquillity" in ICH and another called "Westford" in UHC. DE 16 gives no other titles, nor does it mention the ICH variant.

76. Pilgrim: SH 150, OSH 201. It is found under this title in KnH, MoH, WestPs, SocH, and AUH. It is called "The Weary Traveller" in ICH, and a similar tune is found under the title "Traveller" in SKyH, AUH, UHC, and WestPs. SF 98 mentions that the tune is to be found in *The Christian Science Hymnal* under the title "King's Lynn."

77. Pisgah: SH 80, OSH 58. This is another popular tune and is to be found under this title in UHC, KnH, GChM, MoH, AUH, ChH, SacMel, LCL, Rev, and WChH. It is called "Mt. Pisgah" in SabB and "Melrose" in SocHTB. SF 123 gives no other names, but DE 279 gives a slightly elaborated version under the title of "The Land for Me." It is also related to "Cleburne," OSH 314, and "Heavenly March," SH 253. See also Chapter IV.

78. Pleasant Hill: SH 66, OSH 205, NH 43. It is to be found under this name in SKyH, UHC, SacMel, WChH, WestPs, KnH, CrH, and SocH. It is called "Zion's Light" in Phil. "Sweet Rivers," SH 166, is very similar. DE 91 gives "Zion's Light" as a variant.

79. Primrose: SH 3, OSH 47. This is another very popular tune, and it is to be found usually under "Primrose," "Twenty-fourth," or "Twenty-fourth Psalm," or as "Chelmsford." It is also sometimes called "Melody" as in PrPs, SoHTB, and PsHSS. In Phil it appears as "Memphis" and Funk's *Choral Music* uses the tune for "Auf, Seele, auf," page 65. DE 165 lists no other titles.

80. Plenary: SH 262, OSH 162. This is "Auld Lang Syne," but Jackson gives it in SF 128. It goes by a variety of titles: "Clover Green" in SKyH, KnH, and AUH, "Fair Haven" in TZ, CrMin, and Phil, "Plenare" in WestPs, and "The Blessings of a Clear Title" in AmVoc. Jackson gives no other titles for it.

81. Ragan: OSH 176. In Rev a similar tune is called "Bound Home." SF 181 gives the alternative title "I Belong to This Band." Both "Ragan" and "Bound Home" are similar to "Tennessee," SH 28.

82. Reflection: NH 13. It is found under this title in UHC, KnH, MoH, and WestPs. In WyRepII a major version of this Mixolydian tune is called "New Canaan." SF 122 gives no other name.

83. Restoration: SH 5, OSH 312. It is found under this name in WChH and WestPs, and under "Beaufort" in ChrCho. SH 239 calls it "I will Arise." DE 69 has a variant called "Hayden." There is a major version of this Aeolian tune in SKyH called "Humble Penitent." SocH has a version in compound meter called "I Love the Lord" which may also be found in DE 200.

84. Rockbridge: SH 8. The tune appears under this title in UHC, KnH, MoH, BH, PrPs, ChH, and SacMel. It is called "Forest" in most northern books, including MeHT, TZ, and SL. This is also given as an alternative title in PrPs. AnS 204 lists this as "Rockbridge" without mentioning the other titles.

85. Rocky Road: OSH 294. Found in DE 266 as "I'm Almost Done Traveling."

86. Sailor's Home: SH 182. SF 6 notes that this is called "Sonnet" in *The Revivalist* of 1868.

87. Saints Bound for Heaven: SH 258, OSH 35. It is also found under this title in WChH. In Rev (1869) it is called "O He's Taken my Feet." DE 247 lists it as "Our Bondage it Shall End."

88. Salvation: SH 8, NH 24. It is found under this name in KnH, UHC, GChM, MoH, AUH, ChH, SacMel, SabB, and GChM. It is called "Tennessee" in HSP and in Funk's *Choral Music* it is set to German words beginning "Was much aus dieser Welt betrubt." SF 95 lists only "Salvation."

89. Samanthra: SH 322. It is to be found under this title in SKyH, AUH, and SacMel (it is called "Samantha" here). In GChM and PrPs it is called "Zion's Pilgrim." DE 119 lists "Samanthra" only.

90. Save Mighty Lord: OSH 70. This is called "Save O Save" in Rev and simply "O Save" in WChH. SH 198 lists it under the OSH title.

91. Soda: SH 331, NH 67. SH gives the alternative title of "Tender Care." SF 121 lists this as "Tender Care." The appearance in NH is not mentioned nor is the alternative title.

92. Soft Music: OSH 323. This is the German folk song "Du, du liegst mir im Herzen," as is duly noted in DE 114. It is called "Home" in SacMel, "Palmyra" in TZ, and "Thou Knowest That I Love Thee" in AmVoc.

93. Solemn Thought: SH 29. The tune is found under this name in

SKyH, UHC, AUH, and KnH, but is called "Sinful Youth" in ICH. SF 145 lists it as "Remember Sinful Youth or Solemn Thought."

94. Solicitude: SH 9. It is to be found under this name in SKyH, MoH, SacMel, and KnH. In ICH it is called "The Lord Will Provide." DE 163 gives the Ingalls reference but does not mention the name.

95. Star in the East: SH 16. It is found under this name in KnH, SacMel, and WestPs, but is called "Hail the Blest Morn" in ChH. DE 182 lists the first title only.

96. Supplication: SH 5. It is to be found under this title in GChM, MoH, AUH, WyRepI, UHC, and SocH. It is called "Seasons" in SacMel and "Ach Gott wie manches Herze leid" in Funk's *Choral Music.* SF 105 mentions no other title.

97. Sweet Canaan: OSH 87. This is simply called "Canaan" in HS. SF 190 gives also "I'm Bound for the Land of Canaan."

98. Sweet Prospect: SH 137, OSH 65. A variant of this tune is given in Rev (1869) as "O Come." AnS 62 gives this. See also DE 197.

99. Teacher's Farewell: OSH 34. This is called "Houston" in ChrCho, "No Sorrow There" in DevHT and SZ, "Dunbar" in PsHSS, "Nearer Home" in SoHTB, "No Parting There" in WChH, and "Heavenly Shore" in JasG. DE 84 gives none of this.

100. Tennessee: SH 28. It is found under this name in SKyH and AUH. A close relative is called "Communion" in SZ, BH, and CrH. It is called "Everlasting Day or Communion" in WChH and another version in the same book is called "Glorious Day." An early version is found in ICH as "Millennium." SF 24 gives the above references.

101. This World is not my Home: SH 293. AnS 92 lists the tune as "Heaven is my Home."

102. To Die no More: OSH 111. This is called "We're Going Home" in SL, "I'm Going Home" in *Epworth Hymnal No. 3,* and simply "Going Home" in HSP, MeHy, and DevHT. SF 74 gives it under the OSH title with a single reference to *Good Old Songs* 363.

103. Travelling Pilgrim: SH 313, OSH 278. This tune is listed in DE 293 as "No More Storm Clouds."

104. True Happiness: SH 127. It is listed thus in WChH but is called "O How Happy are They" in Rev. DE 125 lists this as "True Happiness."

105. Villulia: OSH 56. This is very like "Invocation" in SH 193. SF 21 gives the alternative title "Bartimeus" and also gives the "Invocation" variant with a reference in *Good Old Songs.* It lists a further variant called "Lord Revive Us."

106. Vernon: SH 34, OSH 95. It appears under this title in SKyH, GChM, SacMel, and WyRepII. An earlier version is found in ICH

as "Farewell Hymn." DE 19 gives no other name for this nor does it mention the ICH version.

107. Warrenton: SH 94, OSH 145, NH 56. This title is also used in WChH. It is called "Pilgrim Stranger" in LZ, TZ, and AmVoc; it is called "Pilgrim" in ChH and "Female Pilgrim" in SacMel and LCL. SF 205 found it under the title "I am Bound for the Kingdom" in *Good Old Songs.* SF also gives "Pilgrim Stranger" and "Female Pilgrim" but in different books from those listed above.

108. Webster: SH 10, OSH 31. It appears under this title in Sac-Mel, SocH, and WChH. In UHC and SKyH it is called "New Hope," and in WestPs it is called "Melody." AnS 230 lists the tune as "New Hope."

109. Wesley: SH 114. This is the same as "Jerusalem" in SH 11 and OSH 53. Under the first title it appears in KnH, MoH, AUH, and WyRepl. Jackson does not include this for it is a fuguing piece, but the melody is definitely folkish.

110. Young Convert: SH 308. It is thus listed in AmVoc and ICH. A closely related tune is "Wonder" in Rev (1869).

The author makes no claim that the above list is complete or even that some tunes have not been missed in the books examined. The list is given simply in the hope that it may be of use to subsequent scholars.

The conclusion must be reached, as Jackson discovered earlier, that many of these tunes were common property and appeared independently of one another in the various books and manuals. A further conclusion may be hazarded after a glance at the bibliography at the end of this chapter—that these tunes were rather more widely known than even Dr. Jackson suspected. In other words, not only were they known to "the folk" but were also widely known among the middle-class members of many Protestant churches. But of this more in the next chapter.

LIST OF ABBREVIATIONS

(Since all of these books appear in the bibliography, only the name and date will be given here for each.)

The three Jackson books referred to are the following:

AnS   Another Sheaf of White Spirituals, 1952
DE   Down East Spirituals and Others, 1943
SF   Spiritual Folk-Songs of Early America, 1937

The hymnals and manuals used are the following:

AmVoc	American Vocalist, editions of 1849 and 1869
AnR	Ancient Harmony Revived, 1850 edition
AUH	American or Union Harmonist, 1831
BapHy	Baptist Hymnal, 1833
BapHT	Baptist Hymn and Tune Book, 1875
BH	Beauties of Harmony, 1814
BHT	Book of Hymns and Tunes, 1874 (Presbyterian)
ChH	Church Harmony, edition of 1841
CHMeCh	A Collection of Hymns for use in the Methodist Episcopal Church, 1811
ChrCho	Christian Choralist, 1864
CHT	Congregational Hymn and Tune Book, 1856
CrH	The Christian's Harp, 1839
CrMin	Christian Minstrel, 1850
DevHT	Devotional Hymn and Tune Book, 1864 (Baptist)
EvM	Evangelical Musick, 1834
GChM	Genuine Church Music, 1832
Harm	The Harmonist, 1832
HesH	Hesperian Harp, 1848
HyMeCh	Hymnal of the Methodist Episcopal Church
HSP	Hymns and Songs of Praise, 1874
HS	Harp of the South, 1853
ICH	Christian Harmony (Ingalls), 1805
JasG	Jasper and Gold
Jub	The Jubilee
KnH	Knoxville Harmony, 1840
LCL	Christian Lyre (Leavitt), 1852
LZ	Lute of Zion, 1853
MeH	Methodist Harmonist, 1833
MeHT	Methodist Collection of Hymns and Tunes, 1849
MeHTC	Methodist Hymn and Tune Collection, 1867
MeHy	Methodist Hymnal, 1886
MoH	Missouri Harmony, 1833
MusI	Musical Instructor, 1818
Phil	The Philharmonia, 1875 (Mennonite Church)
PresPs	Presbyterian Psalmodist, 1851
PsC	Psalmodist's Companion, 1793
PsHSS	Psalms and Hymns and Spiritual Songs, 1875
Rev	The Revivalist, edition of 1869
SabB	The Sabbath Bell
SacMel	Sacred Melodian, 1849
SL	Sacred Lute, 1864
SKyH	Supplement to The Kentucky Harmony, edition of 1825
SocH	Social Harp, 1868
SoHTB	Social Hymn and Tune Book, 1863
SSBC	Service of Song for Baptist Churches, 1872
SSPW	Songs for Social and Public Worship, 1867
SSS	Selection of Spiritual Songs, 1881
SZ	Songs of Zion, 1824
TZ	Timbrel of Zion, 1854
UHC	Union Harmony (Caldwell), 1837
UHH	Union Harmony (Holden), 1793
VH	Village Harmony, 1818

Vic	The Victory, 1889
WChH	Christian Harmony (Walker)
WestPs	Western Psalmodist, 1853
WL	Western Lyre, 1833
WyRep	Repository of Sacred Music (Wyeth) Parts I and II, 1820
ZH	Zion's Harp, 1824

XII

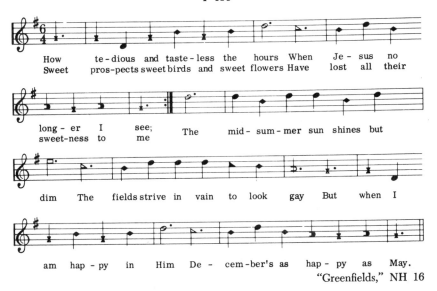

How te-dious and taste-less the hours When Je-sus no
Sweet pros-pects sweet birds and sweet flowers Have lost all their

long - er I see; The mid - sum-mer sun shines but
sweet-ness to me

dim The fields strive in vain to look gay But when I

am hap - py in Him De - cem-ber's as hap - py as May.

"Greenfields," NH 16

THE WRITER can remember her grandmother singing "Greenfields" as the lady bustled about the big kitchen in Hiawatha, Kansas. This would have been in the years before 1912. As a matter of fact, "Greenfields" was included in the Methodist Hymnal of 1935, which was edited by the American hymnologist Robert Guy McCutcheon. Yet "Greenfields" is a bona fide folk hymn, and you can find out all about it in Jackson's *Spiritual Folk-Songs of Early America,* No. 60.

Was the singing of folk hymns always confined to "the folk," that is, country people of relatively low educational and economic status? Dr. Jackson leaves us in some doubt as to this. He acknowledges the importance of Ingalls' *Christian Harmony* of 1805 and *The Revivalist* some sixty years later as showing that these folk hymns were well known in the North throughout the nineteenth century, thus indicating that the knowledge of the tunes was not confined to the southern uplands as he had first thought. In telling how he arrived at the criteria by which he judged a tune's folk origin, he says, "When an example of the old un-written music made its way into the authorized church hymnals—as happened to a *restricted degree* from 50 to 75 years ago—it was called a 'Western Melody' or a 'Southern Melody.' Such designations became an-other reliable token of folk origin."[1] The italics are this author's. True, only about 10 per cent of the tunes covered in this study are to be found in the standard hymnals of the nineteenth century, but 10 per cent is, after all, 10 per cent, and many of these tunes seem to have been very well known indeed.

However, the present writer is interested neither in supporting nor re-futing Dr. Jackson's views but rather in attempting to find out the ex-tent to which the "old music" (that is, both Early American and folk hymns) was known in the nineteenth century among the average middle-class population.

The first bit of evidence that much of the music now restricted to the Old Harps was once in common usage comes from a book to be found in many public libraries. (At least it is in both the Lawson McGhee Li-brary in Knoxville and the Central Library in Indianapolis.) This is *The Story of the Hymns and Tunes,* a combination of two earlier books, *The Story of the Hymns* and *The Story of the Tunes,* by Hezekiah But-terworth. The combination (and revision) was made by Theron Brown in 1906. Though no tunes are printed, the description of the tune or the given composer corresponds in the following cases to things in the three Old Harp books used in this study:

1. All Saints New, p. 513, is described as being by "Amariah Hall, 1811" and having the words "O if my Lord would come and meet." OSH 444 has the title and the same words. The composer is given as "Americk Hall, 1811."

2. Anthem for Easter is described on p. 474 as the work of "an ama-teur genius," William Billings, 1785. The key is given as A major. OSH 236 has same key and same date, and Billings is given as com-poser. SH has the same key and composer; NH is in the same key though no composer is given.

3. Bower of Prayer: this is discussed on p. 147; the composer is given as Elder John Osborne and the date as about 1815. The tune is de-scribed as "legato," and "apparently the music was arranged from a flute interlude in one of Haydn's themes." The words are also given. In OSH 100 the composer is given as "Rev. John Osborn, 1815" and the words are the same. In SH 70 the tune and words

1. *Spiritual Folk-Songs,* p. 13.

are the same as in OSH, but the composers are given as Richerson and Walker. They probably arranged it.

4. Bruce's Address, pp. 335–36, gives the air as "Scots what hae wi' Wallace Bled" and adds "or Bruce's Address, as it was commonly called." The words given are different from those in NH 109 and SH 132, but the tune is obviously the same.

5. China, p. 194: "It [China] was composed by Timothy Swan when he was about 26 years of age (1784)." The words given are "Why do we mourn departed friends?" The same words are used in SH 276, though NH 39 has different ones.

6. Coronation, pp. 27 and 59: since this tune has remained in hymnals to the present day and has always been associated with Holden, there can be no doubt that it is the same as the tune called "Old Coronation." The author is given as Holden and the tune has the familiar words.

7. Devotion, p. 514: the composer is given as Amariah Hall. OSH 48 again gives "Amarick Hall, bout 1811."

8. Teacher's Farewell: this is listed as "Dunbar" on p. 531. It is called an "old revival tune" usually associated with the words of Phillip Phillips' "Nearer Home." Note that both "Dunbar" and "Nearer Home" are given as titles in no. 99 in the preceding chapter.

9. Eden of Love, pp. 272–73: "This song, written early in the last century by John J. Hicks, recalls the name of the eccentric traveling evangelist, Lorenzo Dow. . . . It was the favorite hymn of his wife, the beloved Peggy Dow. . . . The words and the tune were printed in Leavitt's Christian Lyre, 1830." No author or composer is given in SH 309, but the words are the same; it is also the same as the LCL version.

10. Garden Hymn, pp. 277–78, "was a common old-time piece sure to be heard at every religious rally. . . . Its vigorous tune is credited to Jeremiah Ingalls." SH 90 has the same words, and elsewhere the tune is credited to Ingalls.

11. Golden Hill, p. 108: "a chime of sweet counterpoint too rare to bury its authorship under the vague phrase 'A Western Melody.'" Since "Golden Hill" is one of the few frequently found tunes that always has the same title, this is sure to be the same as NH 81.

12. Sweet Affliction: this appears under the title "Greenville" on p. 112, "the production of that brilliant but erratic genius and free-thinker, Jean Jaques Rousseau . . . from the opera Le Devin du Village, written about 1752." OSH 145 gives the composer as John J. Rousseau and the date as 1752. *The Story of the Hymns and Tunes* goes on to say, "It is almost a pardonable exaggeration to say that every child in Christendom knows Greenville."

13. Happy Land, p. 304, under the section on Sunday School Hymns: "It is a Hindoo Air arranged by Andrew Young of Edinburgh." OSH 354 says "Andrew Young, 1800."

14. Hosanna, p. 514: the composer is given as Amariah Hall. OSH 178, as usual, gives the first name as "Americk."

15. Ninety-third: this is listed as "Kentucky." (See Chapter XI, no. 70.) "Old Kentucky, by Jeremiah Ingalls. Sung as a solo by a sweet and spirited voice, it slightly resembled Golden Hill." (It does.) OSH 31 also attributes this tune to Jeremiah Ingalls.

16. Lenox, p. 395: "the clarion melody of Edson's 'Lenox' to Wesley's 'Blow ye the trumpet blow'. . . ." These words are associated with all three Old Harp versions (SH 77, OSH 40, NH 42) and it is always attributed to Edson or Lewis Edson.

17. Loving Kindness, p. 277: "The tune, with its queer curvet in every second line . . . was probably a camp-meeting melody in use for some time before its publication. It is found in Leavitt's Christian Lyre as early as 1830. The name 'William Caldwell' is all that is known of its composer, though he is supposed to have lived in Tennessee." The above description fits the tune, and, though NH 28 does not give the composer, elsewhere the tune is attributed to Caldwell. This is probably the William Caldwell of *The Union Harmony* printed in Maryville, Tennessee, in 1837. "Loving Kindness" appears in this book.

18. Majesty, p. 16: it is attributed here to William Billings, and of course OSH 291 attributes it to the same composer.

19. Mear: on p. 130 it is said that this tune is sometimes attributed to a Scotsman, Aaron Williams, who lived in London, but that another account "and the more probable one" gives an American origin to the tune. "It is found in a small New England collection of 1726, but is not in any English or Scottish collection. 'Mear' is presumably an American tune." See discussion of this tune in Chapter II.

20. Montgomery: p. 35, "In the memories of very old men and women who sang the fugue music of Morgan's 'Montgomery'. . . ." As we have seen in Chapter II, though this is attributed to "More" in NH 158, it is undoubtedly by Justin Morgan. The words in NH are the same as those given by *The Story.*

21. Mullins: it is called "Nettleton" on p. 112. See no. 68, Chapter XI. *The Story* attributes the tune to Wyeth (1810) and gives it as the tune most commonly associated with the words "Come Thou Fount of Every Blessing." These words are still associated with the tune in the more evangelical hymnals of today. OSH 323 attributes the tune to Elder Dumas, but it is "Nettleton" all right.

22. New Jerusalem: on pp. 506–7 the work is ascribed to Jeremiah

Ingalls, and that it "is sung now only as a reminiscence of the music of the past, at church festivals, charity fairs, and entertainments of similar design, but the action and heart joy of it always evoke sympathetic applause." OSH 299 has the same words and also ascribes it to Ingalls.

23. Northfield: on p. 507, "Northfield is still in occasional use, and it is a jewel of a melody."

24. Ode on Science, p. 330: This tune was "the favorite of village assemblies and the inevitable practice-piece for amateur violinists." Further information was given in Chapter II, no. 44.

25. Pisgah, p. 118: "an old revival piece by J. C. Lowry (1820), once much heard in camp-meetings, but it is a pedestrian tune with too many quavers and a headlong tempo." OSH 58 gives "J. C. Lowry, 1820."

26. Restoration, p. 514: this is not the same "Restoration" that is mentioned in the chapter on folk hymns; there are two tunes with this name in OSH. This one is credited in OSH 271 to "Americh Hall, 1811." *The Story* gives the composer as Amariah Hall but mentions no date.

27. Russia, p. 466: Daniel Reed is given as the composer here and in OSH 107.

28. Salem: there is some doubt about this. *The Story* says that the name of the composer is uncertain, but that it was "in the old *Psalmist.*" It also says that the tune is in 6/8 and the words given are in L.M. OSH 68 gives the tune as being from the *Psalmist* and it is a tune in L.M., but the meter is a misbarred 3/2. SH 12, also called "Salem," is in 6/4 but the tune is C.M., not L.M. Neither has a composer given.

29. Sherburne: this one is unmistakable. *The Story* gives Read as the composer and mentions that this was the first American musical setting of "While Shepherds Watched." Both words and composer are the same in OSH 186.

30. Windham, pp. 407–8: Read is given as the composer, and the tune is said to be in minor. OSH 38 gives "Daniel Read, 1785" as composer, and the tune is certainly in minor.

So much for the evidence of *The Story of the Hymns and Tunes.* Thirty tunes which, with the exception of "Coronation," are now known only to Old Harp singers seem to have been familiar enough to our great-grandparents to be included in what was apparently a standard work of reference. Of these, sixteen were Early American and fourteen were folk hymns. There may have been other folk hymns included in the work, but, owing first to the multitudinous names under which a folk hymn may be known and owing also to the fact that *The Story* does not contain music, it is impossible to tell.

Let us look next at a perfectly respectable hymnal, that of the Methodist Episcopal Church for 1849. The full title is *The Methodist Collection of Hymns and Tunes*.

It is a fine hymnal. My copy, rescued from the furnaces of the Roberts Park Methodist Church in Indianapolis, is bound in leather and has ecclesiastical designs on back, front, and spine. It has 352 pages, not counting the indices and prefaces, containing 307 tunes, many of which serve for more than one text. Some of these tunes are tried-and-true favorites still in use: "Arlington," "St. Ann's," "Pleyel's Hymn," and the more popular tunes of Lowell Mason and Thomas Hastings. Fifty-one of the tunes also appear in one or the other (sometimes all three) of the Old Harp books forming the basis of this study. Among these are twelve folk hymns and ten Early American. In addition there is one tune attributed to Read and another to Billings which are not in these particular Old Harps. There is also one folk hymn not in these books.

The Early American tunes are the following:

1. Bridgewater	6. Lenox
2. China	7. Lisbon
3. Concord	8. Mear
4. Coronation	9. Northfield
5. Greenfield	10. Winter

The folk hymns, given first by the titles in the Methodist hymnal and then by their Old Harp names, are these:

1.	Bartimeus	Charlestown
2.	Chelmsford	Primrose
3.	Confidence	Confidence
4.	Contrast	Greenfields
5.	Dunlap's Creek	Dunlap's Creek
6.	Forest	Rockbridge
7.	Golden Hill	Golden Hill
8.	Gospel Trumpet	Gospel Trumpet
9.	Greenville	Sweet Affliction, Importunity
10.	Kentucky	Ninety-third
11.	Nettleton	Mullins
12.	Willoughby	Happy Matches

It is needless to say that the harmony of these is the perfectly correct European harmony of the day.

Another hymnal, from a different denomination, is *The Presbyterian Psalmodist,* "A Collection of Tunes Adapted to the Psalms and Hymns of the Presbyterian Church in the United States of America." It had its beginnings in the General Assembly of 1848, when a committee was appointed, to quote from the "Advertisement" at the beginning of the book, "to take into consideration the subject of Church Music, with special reference to the preparation of a book of tunes adapted to our present Psalmody." This committee reported to the General Assembly the following year and was empowered to go ahead with the compilation of a new hymnal. Thomas Hastings was appointed editor, and the book was finally published, through the Board of Publication of the church, in 1851. Thomas Hastings, the albino musician, had taught singing schools in his youth, but, coming under the influence of Lowell Mason, he became one of what Dr. Jackson used to call "the better music boys." Eventually he came to be as influential in New York as was Lowell Mason in Boston. In other words, Hastings was not the man to favor old camp-meeting and revival songs or the harmonic inaccuracies of Billings and his ilk. Nevertheless, the "Advertisement," in explaining "the principles by which we were guided," after mentioning that they wished (1) to retain the old standard tunes and (2) to add new tunes of a worthy character, goes on to say, "3. To insert some tunes which appeared to be favorites in some considerable sections. We desired not to forget that we were making provision for the edification of a large community of various tastes. While we desired to insert only music of such a character as might elevate and improve the standard of taste throughout the Church, we did not feel at liberty to discard such tunes as, after all, might be approved by a better judgment than our own, especially such as were endeared by long and hallowed association and would be extensively and painfully missed from the collection.*" The asterisk refers to a note at the bottom of the page which tells us that "The more ungrammatical tunes of this character are inserted in an appendix."

Of the 314 pages in the body of the book (there is a section of simple anthems and another of chants), there are 95 tunes that appear in one or more of our three Old Harp books. In the despised appendix nine tunes are listed; unfortunately a page is missing from the copy available to the author, but the five tunes present are all in the three Old Harp books of this study. Of the remaining four, one would guess that, on title, all except one are to be found in the books.

Early American tunes are the following:

1. Amherst	9. Majesty
2. Bridgewater	10. Mear
3. China	11. Mount Pleasant
4. Coronation	12. Ninety-fifth
5. Enfield	13. Northfield
6. Georgia	14. Symphony (Morgan)
7. Jordan (Billings)	15. Windham
8. Lenox	16. Winter

The folk hymns will be shown in Table 1.

With these two as a start, other hymnals of the Methodist, Baptist, and Presbyterian churches were examined. They were the following:

1. The New Hymn and Tune Book, 1867. Methodist. New York.
2. Hymnal of the Presbyterian Church, 1867. Philadelphia.
3. The Presbyterian Hymnal, 1874. Philadelphia. (Presbyterian USA).
4. The Book of Hymns and Tunes, 1874. Richmond, Virginia. (Presbyterian, US).
5. The Baptist Hymn and Tune Book, 1875.
6. The Baptist Hymnal, 1883. Philadelphia. (American Baptist).
7. Hymnal of the Methodist Episcopal Church, 1886. Cincinnati.
8. Baptist Hymn and Praise Book, 1904. Nashville. (Southern Baptist).
9. Methodist Hymnal, 1905.

Table 1 shows the incidence of folk hymns in each of these books. It also shows the varying titles under which each tune appears. It must be emphasized that the illustrations in the table are all from standard hymnals of large and recognized churches and were intended to be used at regular worship services, usually the more formal morning service.

TABLE 1

Harp Books	1851 PresPs	1867 NewH&TBk
1. Bruce's Address		
2. Charlestown	Bartimeus	Bartimeus
3. Confidence		Grace
4. Consolation	Hiding Place	

TABLE 1—*Continued*

Harp Books	1851 *PresPs*	1867 *NewH&TBk*
5. Cookham		
6. Crucifixion		
7. Davis		
8. Devotion	The Penitent	
9. Dunlap's Creek	Dunlap's Creek	Dunlap's Creek
10. Elysian		Greenwood
11. Fiducia	Fiducia	
12. Garden Hymn		
13. Golden Hill	Golden Hill	Golden Hill
14. Greenfields	DeFleury	Contrast
15. Happy Day		
16. Happy Matches		Willoughby
17. Holy Manna		
18. Importunity	Greenville	
19. Interrogation		
20. Joyful		
21. Jordan		
22. Kambia	Kambia	
23. King of Peace		
24. Long Time Ago		
25. Loving Kindness	Loving Kindness	
26. Middlebury		
27. Middleton		Harmony Grove
28. Mullins		
29. New Hosanna		
30. Ninety-third	Kentucky	Kentucky
31. Olney		
32. Parting Hand		
33. Pisgah		
34. Primrose	Melody or Chelmsford	Chelmsford
35. Protection		
36. Restoration		
37. Rockbridge	Rockbridge or Forest	Forest
38. Rockingham	Rockingham	
39. Salvation		
40. Samanthra	Zion's Pilgrim	
41. To Die No More		
42. Teacher's Farewell		No Sorrow There

1867 *HyPresCh*	1874 *PresHyUSA*	1874 *BHT*
1.		
2. Bartimeus		Bartimeus
3.		
4.		
5.		

TABLE 1—*Continued*

	1867 *HyPresCh*	1874 *PresHyUSA*	1874 *BHT*
6.			
7.			
8.			
9.			Dunlap's Creek
10.			
11.			
12.			
13.	Golden Hill	Golden Hill	Golden Hill
14.		DeFleury	DeFleury
15.			
16.			
17.			Hallelujah
18.		Importunity	
19.			
20.			
21.			
22.			
23.			Greenville
24.			
25.			Loving Kindness
26.			
27.			Solon
28.			
29.			
30.		Kentucky	Kentucky
31.			
32.			
33.			Pisgah
34.		Melody	Chelmsford
35.			Protection
36.			
37.		Forest	Forest
38.			
39.	Salvation		Salvation
40.			
41.			
42.			

	1875 *BapHT*	1883 *BapHy*	1886 *HyMeCh*
1.	Bruce		Caledonia
2.	David		
3.			
4.	Pearl		
5.			
6.	Edellium		
7.		Dulcimer	Meditation

TABLE 1—*Continued*

	1875 *BapHT*	1883 *BapHy*	1886 *HyMeCh*
8.			
9.	Dunlap's Creek		
10.	Ives	Beulah	Beulah
11.			
12.		Garden	
13.	Golden Hill		
14.		DeFleury	Contrast
15.		Happy Day	
16.	Willowby	Willoughby	
17.			
18.	Greenville	Greenville	Greenville
19.			
20.	Amazing Grace		
21.			
22.			
23.	Hyacinth		
24.		Ashmore	
25.	Loving Kindness	Loving Kindness	
26.	Happiness	Happiness	
27.			
28.		Nettleton	
29.		Hosanna	
30.	Kentucky or Iowa		Kentucky
31.			
32.			Fillmore
33.			
34.	Melody	Melody	Melody
35.	Bartimeus		
36.			
37.			
38.			
39.			
40.			
41.			
42.			

	1904 *BapH&PBk*	1905 *MethHy*
1.		Caledonia
2.		
3.		
4.		
5.	Cookham	
6.		
7.		Meditation
8.	Pity	
9.		
10.		
11.		

TABLE 1—*Continued*

1904 *BapH&PBk*	1905 *MethHy*
12.	
13. Golden Hill	
14. DeFleury	Contrast
15. Happy Day	Happy Day
16.	
17. Holy Manna	
18.	
19. Interrogation	
20.	
21. Promised Land	
22.	
23.	
24.	
25. Loving Kindness	Loving Kindness
26.	
27. Carroll	
28.	Nettleton
29.	
30. Kentucky	
31. Olney	
32.	Fillmore
33. Pisgah	
34. Melody	
35. Convention	Foundation
36. I Will Arise	
37.	
38.	
39.	
40.	
41. Going Home	Going Home
42. Dunbar	

But the standard hymnals contain only a small percentage of the religious music "everybody knew." The folk hymns came into their own in the revival meetings.

Mrs. Trollope, in her three and one-half years in the states, had ample occasion to observe the revival, both in cities such as Cincinnati and Baltimore and in the rural camp meetings.[2] The point is that everyone—with the exception of Catholics, Episcopalians, Jews, and Quakers—went to revival meetings. "The Revival" was the high spot in the year, both in a religious and in a social sense, and, in at least the smaller cities and the towns, this continued to be the case right up to the time of the First World War. The author remembers many of them, and very har-

2. Mrs. Frances Trollope, *Domestic Manners of the Americans* (1832), Chapters VIII, XI, XV.

rowing they were. Of course by my day the folk hymns had largely been replaced by the gospel songs, some of which had a ragtime beat, some of which were sentimental. Nevertheless, though I cannot associate a specific tune with a specific event, I find that I know quite a few tunes that Jackson classifies as folk hymns. Beside "Greenfields" before mentioned, I seem to have been familiar all my life with "Happy Land," "Importunity," "Loving Kindness," and "Pisgah." I strongly suspect that these were sung around the house by my mother and grandmother, for both were great singers and great pillars of the church.

Dr. Jackson, in the Introduction to *Spiritual Folk-Songs of Early America*, speaks of *The Revivalist* of 1868 as "a veritable treasure trove of the same sorts of song" (i.e., folk hymns). *The Revivalist* was published in Troy, New York, and by 1869 the publisher Joseph Hillman noted that "The demand for The Revivalist has been so great that the publisher has deemed it best to revise and enlarge it for this edition. Sixteen thousand copies have been published in less than a year."[3] This edition further bears a letter from Professor Philip Phillips, musical editor of the Methodist Book Concern, endorsing the work. The 1869 edition contains fifty-three folk hymns that are included in the three books forming the basis of this study. These are given in Table 2.

TABLE 2

Old Harp	*Revivalist*
1. All is Well	All is Well
2. Bower of Prayer	Bower of Prayer
3. Bruce's Address	Caledonia
4. Confidence	Parting
5. Charlestown	Bartimeus
6. Clamanda	Far from my Thoughts
7. Condescension	Return
8. Church's Desolation	Hallowed Spot
9. Davis	Beloved
10. Deep Spring	Land of Rest
11. Elysian	Ives
12. Fiducia	Amazing Grace
13. Golden Hill	Golden Hill
14. Garden Hymn	Garden Hymn
15. Greenfields	DeFleury
16. Grieved Soul	Come my Brethern
17. Good Old Way	All the Way Long
18. Happy Matches	Willowby

3. Note in the 1869 edition.

TABLE 2—*Continued*

Old Harp	*Revivalist*
19. Highlands of Heaven	Sinner's Invitation
20. Holy Manna	Gospel Power; Jesus Calls You
21. Imandra	How Firm a Foundation
22. Indian's Farewell	When Shall we all Meet Again
23. Importunity (Sweet Affliction)	Light Breaks O'er Thee
24. Jordan's Shore	On the Other Side of Jordan
25. Joyful	Coburn; Parting Hymn
26. King of Peace	Lovest Thou Me
27. Kingwood	Pilgrim's Happy Lot
28. Land of Rest	Believer
29. Long Time Ago	Long Time Ago
30. Lover of the Lord	You Must be a Lover of the Lord
31. Meditation	Peace
32. Mercy's Free	Mercy's Free
33. Messiah	Usher
34. Morning Trumpet	Bates
35. Ninety-third	Kentucky
36. Parting Hand	And Can it Be
37. Pastoral Elegy	Corydon
38. Pisgah	Pisgah
39. Ragan	Band Hymn
40. Restoration	I Will Arise
41. Resurrected	Away Over Jordan
42. Royal Proclamation	Royal Proclamation
43. Saints Bound for Heaven	O He's Taken my Feet
44. Saint's Bound for Heaven	Save, Save
45. Something New	Something New
46. Sweet Prospect	O Come O Come
47. Teacher's Farewell	No Sorrow There
48. To Die No More	We're Going Home
49. True Happiness	O Happy are They
50. Union	Union Hymn
51. Warrenton	Pilgrim Stranger
52. Washington	Harris
53. Young Convert	Wonder

Still another indication of the popularity of these tunes among the general public is furnished by the many little books of hymns designed for "Social and Private Devotions." Many of these have the most impeccable origins: *The Social Hymn and Tune Book* was issued by the Presbyterian Publication Committee. The ninth edition, "of 2500 each," was published in Philadelphia, presumably in 1865. Another of the same sort is "Songs of Zion, enlarged, a manual of the best and most popular Hymns and Tunes for social and Private devotion. Published by The American Tract Society, New York, 1864." Other books of this kind that were examined were the following:

1. *Sacred Songs for Family and Social Worship,* "comprising the most approved spiritual hymns with chaste and popular tunes." American Tract Society, New York, 1842.

2. *Temple Melodies,* "About 200 popular tunes . . . selected with special reference to public, social and private worship" by Darius E. Jones. Mason and Law, New York, 1852.

3. *Social Hymns and Tunes* "for Prayer and Social Meetings" by Reverend George C. Robinson. Poe and Hitchcock, Cincinnati, 1863.

4. *Devotional Hymn and Tune Book* "for Social and Public Worship." William Bradbury. American Baptist Publication Society, Philadelphia, 1864.

5. *Songs for Social and Public Worship,* revised edition. "Edited and compiled by the Reverend Edward N. Kirk, D.D." Henry Holt, Boston, 1867.

6. *A Selection of Spiritual Songs* "with music for use in Social Meetings, 5th edition," Reverend Charles S. Robinson, D.D. The Century Company, New York, 1881.

7. *Laudes Domini,* "a selection of Spiritual Songs ancient and modern, for use in the prayer meeting." Charles S. Robinson. The Century Company, New York, 1890.

All of the above books were found in the storerooms of the Maryville College Library in Maryville, Tennessee. Maryville is affiliated with the Presbyterian Church in the USA, i.e., the "northern" branch of the church. It was founded in 1819, and these books are from the libraries of various professors and ministers who were connected with it. The point is simply, again, that educated people used these books and knew these songs. Table 3 shows the incidence of folk hymns in these books. They were much smaller than regular hymnals; most of them were about the size of a prayer book and could be carried in a pocket. The description of *Temple Melodies*—"About 200 popular tunes"—gives some idea as to the number of tunes contained in each.

TABLE 3

Old Harp	1842 SSFSW	1852 TemMel
1. Charlestown	Bartimeus	Bartimeus
2. Cookham		
3. Davis		
4. Devotion		
5. Dunlap's Creek		
6. Elysian		

TABLE 3—Continued

Old Harp	1842 SSFSW	1852 TemMel
7. Garden Hymn		
8. Golden Hill	Golden Hill	Golden Hill
9. Greenfields		DeFleury
10. Happy Matches		
11. Holy Manna		
12. Importunity	Greenville	Greenville
13. Joyful		
14. King of Peace		Lovest Thou Me
15. Long Pilgrim		
16. Long Time Ago		
17. Loving Kindness		Loving Kindness
18. Middlebury		
19. New Britain		
20. Ninety-third		Iowa
21. Parting Hand		
22. Pisgah		
23. Primrose		
24. Rockbridge	Forest	
25. Teacher's Farewell		
26. To Die No More		
27. Warrenton		

1863 SocH&T	1864 SZ*	1864 DevH&T
1. Bartimeus		Bartimeus
2.		
3.	Dulcimer	
4.		
5.		Dunlap's Creek
6. Ives	Beulah	Elysian
7.		Garden Hymn
8.	Golden Hill	Golden Hill
9. DeFleury	DeFleury	DeFleury
10. Willoughby		
11.		
12.		Greenville
13.		Canaan
14.		
15.		
16.	It is Finished	
17. Loving Kindness	Loving Kindness	Loving Kindness
18. Joy		
19.		
20. Iowa	Kentucky	Iowa
21.		
22. Mt. Pisgah		
23.	Melody	Melody
24.		Forest
25.	No Sorrow There	No Sorrow There
26. I'm Going Home		I'm Going Home
27.		

TABLE 3—*Continued*

1865 SocH&TBk	1867 SSPW	1881 SSS	1890 LD
1. Bartimeus	Bartimeus	Bartimeus	Bartimeus
2. Redeeming Love			
3.	Dulcimer		
4. The Penitent			
5. Dunlap's Creek			
6. Ives		Beulah	Beulah
7. Garden	Garden		
8. Golden Hill	Golden Hill		Golden Hill
9. DeFleury			
10.	Willoughby	Willoughby	
11. Bellenden	Bellenden		
12. Greenville	Greenville	Greenville	Greenville
13.			
14.			
15.	Pilgrim		
16.			
17.	Loving Kindness	Loving Kindness	Loving Kindness
18.			
19. Harmony Grove			
20. Iowa		Iowa	Iowa
21.		And Can It Be	
22. Melrose			
23. Melody		Melody	Melody
24. Forest		Forest	
25. Nearer Home	No Sorrow There°°	Dunbar	Dunbar
26.	I'm Going Home		
27.	Pilgrim		

°*Songs of Zion* has one other folk hymn that is not in any of the three books used for this study. *The Devotional Hymn and Tune Book* has six.
°°This tune is also called "Paradise" in SSPW. SSPW has one other folk hymn; SSS has three.

And what of the Early American compositions in these books? There are not too many, possibly because these books are small, and, generally speaking, the fuguing pieces and anthems are quite long. Consequently, any Early American examples in these little books are apt to be either hymn tunes or the shorter fuguing pieces. Thus it is that *Social Hymns and Tunes* of 1863 contains only "Lenox," "China," and "Windham"; *The Devotional Hymn and Tune Book* has these three plus "Northfield" and "Wells." *Laudes Domini* has only "China."

One final item in this chapter. This is *Fillmore's Christian Choralist* which was found in the Butler University storeroom. It was designed to be used either in the singing school or in the home, and, though it was published simultaneously in Philadelphia and Cincinnati, it was probably planned for use in the North since it uses scale numbers instead of shaped notes. Its date is 1864. In it are many folk hymns, often in new variants and with new names:

1. Amboy is "Clamanda."
2. Anderson is "Middleton."
3. Beaufort is "Restoration."
4. Butler is related to "Parting Hand."
5. Burgess is "O Sing to Me of Heaven."
6. Cookham
7. Carman is related to "Lone Pilgrim."
8. Chase is "Pilgrim."
9. Clarington is related to "Lovely Story."
10. Chatterton is "Columbus."
11. Canaan is related to "Sweet Canaan."
12. Dunlap's Creek
13. Etivini is "Highlands of Heaven."
14. Greenfield is "Greenfields."
15. Golden Hill
16. Greenville
17. Goodwin is "Garden Hymn."
18. Hosanna is "New Hosanna."
19. Hiding Place is related to "Consolation."
20. Haskell is "Weary Soul."
21. Houston is "Teacher's Farewell."
22. Idumea
23. Imandra
24. Independence is "Bruce's Address."
25. Infancy is "Consolation."
26. Ives is "Elysian."
27. Kentucky is "Ninety-third."
28. Loving Kindness
29. Leander
30. Lyster is "Parting Hand."
31. Nelson is "Condescension."
32. Nebraska is "Indian's Farewell."
33. Parrish is "Nettleton."
34. Panoply is "Joyful."
35. Primrose
36. Paxan is "Soft Music."
37. Pisgah

38. Rockingham
39. Rockbridge
40. Superior is "Plenary."
41. Saint's Sweet Home is "Home."
42. Salem
43. Valle is "Davis."
44. Union Hymn is "Union."
45. White Pilgrim is "Lone Pilgrim."
46. Wolfe is "Deep Spring."
47. Wallace is "King of Peace."

In addition this book contains at least twelve more folk hymns that either are not in the three books used in this study or else were such remote variants that I hesitated to include them in the above list.

The book is also fairly well supplied with things from Early America: Bridgewater, Concord, Coronation, Easter Anthem, Lenox, Northfield, Suffield, Windham.

Some mention has already been made of where the books came from that are used in this and some of the other chapters. The rarer ones, of course, had to be used in libraries; but the hymnals, northern singing school manuals, and books of spiritual songs were dug out of the storerooms of churches and libraries and were brought to me by my university pupils. I cannot believe, therefore, that these were used exclusively by "the folk." In fact, as the reader may have suspected by now, the whole point of this chapter is to suggest that quite a few Protestant Americans who lived in the nineteenth century were quite familiar with what today is known as "Old Harp music."

XIII

But above all, those judicious Collectors of bright parts and flowers and observanda's are to be nicely dwelt on; by some called the sieves and boulters of learning; tho' it is left undetermined, whether they dealt in pearls or Meal; and consequently whether they are more value to that which passed thro' or what staid behind.

Swift, *Tale of a Tub*

The recapitulation normally contains all the material of the exposition. . . .

Apel, *Harvard Dictionary of Music*
"Sonata Form"

WHETHER the preceding chapters have dealt in pearls or meal is something that the reader will have to decide for himself. But, lest that reader have lost track of the points made, this penultimate chapter proposes, in the best tradition of the classic sonata, to sum up the essentials that have gone before.

As the subtitle of this book notes, the main emphasis is on, first, the folk hymns, and second, the Early American compositions. The remaining materials in the books, the English and Scottish psalm tunes, the many hymns by Lowell Mason and his contemporaries and by English writers, even the more modern fuguing pieces and anthems of "folk" origin, have been very lightly stressed. (Fuguing pieces of later date sometimes show evidence of dyadic harmony depending on the composer. Some measures from such fuguing pieces have been used in occasional illustrations.) Furthermore, there are a good many tunes in each of the books that defy classification; one never sees them in other manuals, and they certainly have none of the characteristics of a folk hymn. They seem utterly without character, and the author cannot remember hearing any of them sung.

Of the two kinds of music discussed, it must be evident that the author is rather more interested in the folk hymns than in the Early American compositions. And so, reverting to Chapter III, how may one recognize a folk hymn? The author, admittedly on rather shaky ground,

believes that the melody of a folk hymn is apt to show certain characteristics, by no means all present in every tune, and that if three or more
of these characteristics are present in a tune and that tune is in an Old
Harp book, one may proceed on the assumption that it is a folk hymn.
These characteristics are as follows:

1. The scale used is more likely than not to be gapped. Pure and
basically pentatonic scales seem to occur more often in "major"
modes (Ionian and Mixolydian) than in the "minor" ones (Aeolian
and Dorian). See both appendices. Furthermore, hexatonic scales
are more apt to add "fa" in major modes and "ti" in minor modes.
Again, see both appendices.
2. There are certain characteristic rhythmic patterns for each
meter. These are given in Chapter III.
3. Folk hymns frequently have mixed meters expressed in time
signatures that are contrary to the accents of the words. Misbarring
is frequent.
4. A large number of folk hymns have a characteristic melodic
shape (that of a triple arch, with the tessitura of the two middle
phrases higher than that of the first and last phrases) or a modification of this shape.
5. The form ABBA or ABB'A (or in six-phrase tunes where the
middle phrases are alike) is almost always indicative of folk origin
although it is by no means common. The typical use of repeated
figures mentioned in Chapter III is found much more frequently.
6. Many folk hymns are centonized to some extent. As Jackson
noted years ago, tunes that are not contrafacti of secular folk
tunes often have phrases that have been borrowed from such
tunes. The author believes that such borrowing may also be made
from other folk hymns, from Early American material, and, in fact,
from almost any material.
7. A refrain of the "Halle, hallelujah" type inserted into an obviously old-time text almost always indicates a folk hymn.

These rather tentative criteria only serve to reinforce an opinion
already indicated in preceding chapters: certain tunes in the Jackson
index are not true folk hymns. The author cannot believe that "Kambia"
is a folk hymn. Nor, on evidence already presented, is "Benevento." The
tunes based on the "Vesper Hymn" are too much like the original to have
been remembered from a long oral tradition; besides the "Vesper Hymn,"
under a variety of names, was in nearly every nineteenth-century hymn
book. "Long Time Ago" must have been included in the singing school

manuals shortly after its appearance as a popular parlor song and before it had a chance to go through a long period of oral transmission. There are a few more, all indicated in Appendix ɪ; for none of these could Jackson find true folk song backgrounds.

This is not to belittle the Jackson achievement. Besides the amount of sheer work involved in compiling the three books, there is the fact that he recognized the Chapin tunes as true folk hymns even though he could find no generating English folk song for several of them and that for at least one other the reference is decidedly farfetched.

As for harmonic characteristics, a comparison of Early American and folk hymn harmonization is in order. Granting that both have certain characteristics in common—the linear aspect, the melody in the tenor— the general differences may be summed up as follows:

Early American

1. Scales used are seven-tone major or minor.
2. The harmonic minor is almost always used.
3. Modulation is used freely, usually to the key of the dominant.
4. Though the writing is contrapuntal and often crude by conventional textbook standards, the harmony is essentially tertian.
5. The functions of the tonic, sub-dominant, and dominant seem to have been understood, particularly at the cadence.

Folk Hymn

1. Though seven-tone scales may be used, gapped scales are far more common, and Dorian and Mixolydian modes are fairly common.
2. The Aeolian minor was used almost exclusively after shaped notes came in and probably was in common use before the time of Little and Smith. Note for instance how awkwardly the raised sevenths occur in the "Shouting Hymn" in Ingalls' *Christian Harmony* (Ex. 28). They seem to have been placed as a matter of duty rather than of musical feeling. It is quite probable that the tune was sung as Aeolian.
3. There is no modulation, not even that implied by melodic lines. In fact, if modulation is indicated, the tune is almost certain to belong outside the folk hymn category.
4. Though the writing may be contrapuntal, the harmony is essentially dyadic. The operative word is "essentially," for an occasional triad creeps in and there is certainly no worked-out system of dyadic harmonization.

5. Though the bass may drop a fourth or rise a fifth at the cadence, the harmony above the next-to-the-last bass note is seldom a clear-cut dominant or dominant seventh. There seems to be no system of dyad progression, even at cadence points, beyond the natural progression of the various voices along the pentatonic scale. Since hexatonic scales are only a step away from the pentatonics, dyadic harmony is frequently used to harmonize hexatonic tunes.

Last, but by no means least, the author believes that folk hymns in general were rather more widely known in the nineteenth century than Jackson realized. Not, perhaps, by the Vanderbilts, the Astors, or the Goulds (although it is quite possible that the senior Rockefeller was acquainted with some of them), but by the solid citizens of the middle income groups, both urban and rural. These were the church-going people of the evangelical Protestant denominations, people who, though they might go to a more or less formal morning service, enjoyed a good old-fashioned revival or kept little books of "Spiritual Songs" for home devotions. It is true that towards the end of the nineteenth century newer books of "Gospel Hymns" replaced the "Spiritual Songs" for prayer meetings and home devotions, but many of the new books contained a few of the older tunes. It goes without saying that the singing school scholars knew the folk hymns; even in the North, where Lowell Mason reigned for a long, long time, nearly every manual contained some of the older music.

It is nice to reflect that this music is perhaps not being entirely abandoned to the Old Harpers. The standard hymnals of today are tending more and more to include a few of the folk hymns. The Episcopal Hymnal of 1940 contains "Land of Rest," "Kedron," a version of "Consolation" called "Morning Song," and a couple of others not in the three books covered in this study. The 1956 Hymnal of the Southern Baptists lists "Amazing Grace," "Holy Manna," "Land of Rest," "Nettleton," and "Pisgah." The last hymnal to be published by the two main branches of the Presbyterians, together with the United Presbyterians and the Reformed Church, contains "Amazing Grace," "Boundless Mercy," "Covenanters," and "Nettleton." The official hymnal of the Methodist Church, copyrighted first in 1964 and again in 1966, outdoes them all by including no less than thirteen folk hymns in the books covered by this study as well as three extra tunes not in these books. This Methodist Hymnal also contains a couple of Early American goodies, "Lenox" (used for two sets of words) and "Windham." "Coronation," of course, occurs in all of these hymnals; indeed, it has been deservedly popular since the day it was written.

It can be argued that the folk hymns never entirely disappeared from the hymnals of the great Protestant denominations. The Baptist Hymnal of 1926 (published jointly by the American Baptist Publication Society and the Sunday School Board of the Southern Baptist Convention) lists "DeFleury," "Foundation," "Happy Day," "Loving Kindness," "Nettleton," and "Pisgah." The Methodist Hymnal of 1935, authorized by both the "northern" and the "southern" branches, contains "Amazing Grace," "Beloved," "Caledonia" (Bruce's Address), "Contrast," "Fillmore" (Parting Hand), "Foundation," and "Nettleton." Even the Presbyterian Hymnal of 1933, a book that draws largely on the English *Hymns Ancient and Modern,* contains "Nettleton."

Unfortunately, these tunes do not seem to be sung much by the congregations in whose hymnals they appear. Episcopalian friends, all regular communicants, say they have never heard "Kedron," "Land of Rest," or "Morning Song." Baptists and Methodists, in this town at least, are unfamiliar with the folk hymns in their hymnals, and up to now I have yet to hear a folk hymn sung in a Presbyterian church.

Times change, and tastes change with them. It is to be hoped that the great Protestant denominations will rediscover the grand old tunes in their hymn books.

XIV

The matter grows in interest. . . .

> A. Conan Doyle, "The Reigate Puzzle"
> (Sherlock Holmes speaking)

✦✦✦✦✦

WHEN THE AUTHOR first began to study the contents of the Old Harp books it was with no further thought than to isolate the Early American compositions in *The New Harp of Columbia*. That was thirty years ago. But, as others besides myself have noted, one damned thing leads to another.

The preceding chapters merely scratch the surface of the problems with which they attempt to deal. In addition, there are a good many other problems upon which one could profitably work. For instance:

Do the fuguing pieces have any connection with the French and Scotch "Psalmes in Reports"?

From what parts of the British Isles did the secular folk songs that generated the folk hymns come? That few came from the West Country, Ireland, or Scotland (except by second hand) is just a personal guess.

Who were some of the more shadowy figures of early American composition: the "Wetmore" of "America," for instance? How much were these men influenced by folk music?

Of course someone ought to go around with a tape recorder before it is too late and note the variations in singing in different parts of the country. Do many groups turn Aeolians into Dorians, or is this just a peculiarity of east Tennessee? The groups that the author has heard in other parts of the South contained a large percentage of younger people who read accurately, but perhaps this is not so in more isolated sections.

British folk song is full of stock phrases and figures. The author has this both from Chapter VII of Sharp's *English Folk-Song: Some Conclusions* and on the word of Miss Maude Karpeles herself. Have many of these stock phrases and figures been carried over into the folk hymns of America? Much more work needs to be done on the subject of centonization.

All these and other like questions the author presents, with best wishes, to younger and no doubt better qualified scholars.

Appendix I

A LIST OF FOLK HYMNS GIVEN IN THE JACKSON BOOKS

SF:	*Spiritual Folk-Songs of Early America*
DE:	*Down East Spirituals and Others*
AnS:	*Another Sheaf of White Spirituals*
✻	Indicates that this tune, in the opinion of this author, is not a true folk hymn.

Tune	SH	OSH	NH	Jackson Reference
1. Ionian (Major) Tunes				
a. Pentatonic or Basically Pentatonic Tunes				
1. Beach Spring (See also "Fount of Glory")		81		SF 56 is the same tune in a different rhythm called "Missionary Farewell"
2. Bellvue (See also "Christian's Farewell and Protection")		72		DE 145
3. Bower of Prayer	70	100		DE 3
4. Carnsville ("The Christians" is given as a second name in SH.)		109		DE 277 is a similar tune called "O Give Him Glory"
5. Christian's Farewell	334			Same as "Bellvue"
6. Christian's Hope (1)	74	134		DE 167
7. Christian's Hope (2)		206		SF 162
8. Christian Soldier (1) (See also "Humility")	45	57		SF 68
9. Christian Soldier (2)	95			AnS 269
10. Christian Prospect	323			SF 161
11. Cleburne (See also "Heavenly March")		314		AnS 91 called "Pilgrim's Band"
12. Complainer	18	141		DE 45
13. Concord	321		46	DE 161
14. Confidence (1)	33			DE 142
15. Contented Soldier (See also "Desire for Piety")	314			DE 217 called "Till the Warfare is Over"
16. Cuba		401		SF 156
17. Day of Judgment	84			AnS 273
18. Deep Spring			93	SF 35
19. Desire for Piety		76		Same as "Contented Soldier"
20. Devotion	13	48		SF 120
21. Done With the World		88		SF 209
22. Dudley	250			AnS 135

185

	A	B	C	Reference
62. New Year	333		67	AnS 318
63. Ninety-third	7	31	25	DE 146
64. Old Ship of Zion		79		SF 191
65. Olney	64	135		DE 70
66. Parting Hand	113	62	95	DE 16
67. Penick		387		SF 85
*68. Penitent's Prayer	290			DE 151
69. Pisgah	80	58		SF 123
70. Pleasant Hill	66	205	43	DE 91
71. Plenary	262	162		SF 128
(See "Hamburg" above)				
72. Promised Day		409		DE 95
73. Prospect	92	30	15	DE 147
74. Protection			57	See "Bellvue" above
75. Ragan		176		SF 181
76. Redeeming Grace	56			DE 6
77. Religion is a Fortune		319		SF 187
78. Resignation	38			DE 94
79. Resurrected		153		SF 178
80. Rockbridge	288			AnS 204
81. Rocky Road		294		DE 266
82. Roll Jordan		274		SF 184
83. Roll On		275		DE 280
84. Romish Lady	82			SF 1
85. Royal Proclamation	146			SF 84
86. Sailor's Home	182			SF 6
87. Salem (2)	12			AnS 255
88. Sawyer's Exit		338		SF 129
89. Service of the Lord		80		SF 215
90. Sincerity	101			AnS 278
91. Sister's Farewell		55		DE 20
92. Something New	254			AnS 185 is somewhat different
93. Sweet Affliction	259	145		See "Importunity" above.
94. Sweet Harmony	59			SF 130 called "O Tell Me No More."
95. Teacher's Farewell		34		DE 84
96. Thorny Desert	83			AnS 250
97. Transport	152			DE 48
98. True Happiness	127			DE 125
99. Victoria		290		SF 229
100. Warrenton	94	145	56	SF 205
101. Weary Soul		72		DE 23
102. Webster	10	31		AnS 230 called "New Hope."

b. Hexatonic Ionian Tunes with "fa"

	A	B	C	Reference
1. Albion	23	52	12	SF 78
2. Animation		103		AnS 92 called "Heaven is my Home."

3. Brooklyn			70	AnS 309
4. Canton			103	SF 64 called
(See also "Interrogation")				"Hark my Soul."
5. Charlestown	23	52		DE 80
6. Davis	15			SF 163
7. Erie			105	DE 68
8. Essay	255	157		AnS 256
9. Farewell (1)			32	SF 25
10. France			148	AnS 329
11. Greenfields	71	127	16	SF 60
12. Grieved Soul		448		DE 71
13. Happy Matches		96		AnS 137
(See also "Willoughby")				
14. Heavenly Port		378		·SF 201
15. Home in Heaven		41	87	AnS 149
(The OSH, NH, and AnS versions are all somewhat different)				
16. Interrogation	249			Same as "Canton" above.
17. Imandra		45		DE 21
18. Imandra New	34			Same as "Imandra"
19. Isles of the South	86			AnS 128
20. Lovely Story		104		AnS 106
21. Lover of the Lord		124		DE 245
22. Marston			131	DE 155
°23. Mear	24	49	14	AnS 311
24. Millenium	75	130		DE 111
25. Pardoning Love	268			AnS 112
26. Pilgrim's Lot	138			AnS 283
27. Primrose	3	47		DE 165
28. Primrose Hill		43		AnS 264
29. Rockingham	300			DE 150
30. Sweet Canaan		87		SF 190
31. Sweet Union		424		AnS 77
32. This World is Not My Home	293			AnS 92
33. Turtle Dove	43			AnS 271
34. Willoughby	277			Same as "Happy Matches" above.

c. Hexatonic Ionian Tunes with "ti"

°1. China	276		39	DE 112
2. Come and Taste	105			DE 231
3. Dunlap's Creek	276			SF 79
4. Dying Californian		410		SF 10
5. Elysian	100	139		DE 78
6. Frozen Heart		93		SF 65
7. Indian Convert	133			Same as "Nashville" below.
8. Lancaster			91	DE 162
9. Legacy	73			AnS 129
10. Liverpool	1	37	113	SF 7

	SH	OSH	NH	Jackson Reference
11. Minister's Farewell	14	69		DE 18
12. Nashville		64		See "Kingwood" Section I-a
13. Old Fashioned Bible		342		AnS 126
14. Passing Away		445		DE 216
15. Saints Bound for Heaven	258	35		DE 247
16. South Union		344		DE 5
17. Sweet Rivers	166	61		DE 88
18. Tennessee	28			SF 24
19. Watchman's Call	65			AnS 175

d. Seven-tone Ionian Tunes

	SH	OSH	NH	Jackson Reference
1. All is Well	306	122		SF 58
*2. Benevento	317		50	AnS 68
3. Cardiphonia			138	AnS 100
4. Convoy			29	AnS 333
5. Crucifixion	25			SF 16
6. Family Circle		333		DE 219
7. Gray Ridge			78	AnS 136
8. Joyful			141	SF 227
9. Living Lamb		309		AnS 201
10. Long Time Ago	313			AnS 313
11. Morality	44		89	DE 138
12. Mount Zion		88		DE 232 called "Praise Him O Christians."
*13. Murillo's Lesson		358		AnS 134
14. Never Part Again	198		74	AnS 191
15. O Come Come Away	144	334		AnS 339
16. Pacolet	106			AnS 285
17. Soft Music		323		DE 114
18. Solicitude	69			DE 163
19. Sudbury			41	AnS 218
*20. Weeping Saviour (2)		310		AnS 236
21. Welch	109			AnS 212

d. Ionian Tunes with a Five-tone Range (do-re-mi-sol)

	SH	OSH	NH	Jackson Reference
1. Canaan's Land		101		AnS 249
2. To Die No More		111		SF 74
3. We'll Soon Be There		97		AnS 83

2. AEOLIAN TUNES

a. Pentatonic and Basically Pentatonic Tunes

Tune	SH	OSH	NH	Jackson Reference
1. Antioch (2)		277		SF 166
2. Arkansas		271		AnS 251

3. Bozrah (See also "Traveller")	39			SF 138
4. Clamanda (See also "Social Band")		42		SF 93
5. Columbus (See also "Hopewell")	55	67		SF 75
6. Detroit	40	39		SF 147
7. Distress	22	32		DE 107
8. Dying Friend		399		DE 58
9. Ecstasy		106		SF 197
10. Fiducia	92			DE 183
11. Fight On		385		DE 188
12. Golden Harp		274		SF 152
13. Good Physician	49			SF 31
14. Help Me to Sing		376		DE 50
15. Hick's Farewell	19			SF 4
16. Holy City		101		AnS 302
17. Hopewell			37	Same as "Columbus" above
18. Idumea	31	47	44	SF 137
19. Meditation (1)	4			SF 109 "Bourbon" is practically the same.
20. Messiah	97	131		DE 105
21. Morning Trumpet	195	85	99	SF 241
22. New Orleans	76			SF 139
23. Pilgrim	150	201		SF 98
24. Praise God		328		SF 106
25. Restoration (1)	5	312		SF 239
26. Salutation	143			SF 36
27. Save Mighty Lord		70		SF 198
28. Sing to Me of Heaven		312	73	DE 205
29. Social Band	112			Same as "Clamanda" above
30. Solemn Thought	29			SF 145
31. Stockwood		118		SF 103
32. Sweet Morning		421		SF 168
33. Traveller (Same as "Bozrah" above)		8		
34. Vernon	34	95		DE 19

b.   Hexatonic Aeolian Tunes with "fa"

1. Exultation	88	DE 118

c.   Hexatonic Aeolian Tunes with "ti"

1. Alabama	116	196	AnS 362
°2. America	27	36	DE 187
3. Captain Kidd	50		SF 142
4. Child of Grace		77	DE 175
5. Consolation	17		DE 135
6. Consolation New	58		DE 131

*7.	Dublin	13		129	AnS 321
8.	Fairfield	48	29		DE 195
9.	French Broad	265			SF 96
10.	Horton		330		DE 59
11.	Imandra	134			DE 126
12.	I'm on my Journey Home		345		AnS 95
13.	Indian's Farewell	25		134	AnS 332
14.	Jefferson	42	148		AnS 297
15.	Jerusalem	11	53		AnS 360
16.	King of Peace	6	74		DE 192
17.	Leander	128	71	61	SF 107
18.	Loving Kindness (2)		275		DE 297
19.	Marietta (See also "Sweet Heaven")			90	DE 116
20.	Marysville	6			AnS 295
21.	Mexico			147	AnS 108
22.	Morning Star	115			AnS 132
23.	Promised Land	51	128	47	SF 246 called "Bound for the Promised Land"
24.	Rhode Island	145			DE 89
25.	Salem (1)	53	68		DE 177
26.	Salvation	84		24	SF 95
27.	Samanthra	322			DE 119
28.	Sardinia	126	296		DE 52
29.	Separation	30			SF 54
30.	Star in the East	16			DE 182
31.	Star of Columbia	260			AnS 127
32.	Summer			122	DE 79
33.	Supplication	5			SF 105
34.	Sweet Heaven		278		Same as "Marietta" above.
35.	Tribulation	119	29		SF 67
36.	Washington	67			SF 52
37.	Wayfaring Stranger		457		SF 40
38.	Weary Pilgrim		326		AnS 298
39.	Weeping Saviour (1)	7	33		SF 146

d.   Seven-tone Aeolian Tunes

1.	American Star		346		AnS 140
2.	Babel's Streams	52	126		DE 180
3.	Cheerful	91			AnS 259
4.	Christian Song	129		185	AnS 169
5.	Edgefield		82		SF 149
6.	Expression		125		AnS 225
7.	Fulfillment		102		AnS 300
*8.	Kambia	154			DE 117
9.	Kedron	3	48	45	SF 57
10.	Mouldering Vine	87			SF 22
11.	Mississippi	148			SF 99
12.	Pastoral Elegy	147			DE 26

13. Seaman			121	AnS 222
14. Spiritual Sailor	41	150		SF 136
15. Union (2)		116		SF 39
16. War Department	94	160		SF 138

Note: Lena, SH 149, OSH 210, is in the harmonic minor.   AnS 310

3.   Mixolydian Tunes

a.   Pentatonic or Basically Pentatonic Mixolydian Tunes

Tune	SH	OSH	NH	Jackson Reference
1. Anticipation			75	DE 238
2. An Address for All	99			SF 29
3. Bruce's Address	132		109	SF 112 called "Friends of Freedom."
4. Christian Contemplation (See also "Faithful Soldier")			48	SF 59
5. Christian Warfare	37	179		DE 2
6. Church's Desolation		89		SF 28
7. Condescension	312			SF 30
8. Cusseta		73		AnS 274
9. Faithful Soldier	122			Same as "Christian Contemplation" above.
10. Louisiana	62	207		DE 140
11. Midnight Cry	32		84	AnS 69
12. Paradise			68	DE 276
13. Weeping Pilgrim		417		SF 176

b.   Mixolydian Tunes with "fa" (some "fas" are appoggiaturi)

1. Bound for Canaan	193	82		DE 268
2. Converted Thief	9	44		SF 23
3. Hallelujah (1)	107	146		SF 225
4. Reflection			13	SF 122
5. Soda (Tender Care) (Both names are given in SH)	331		67	SF 121
6. White		288		SF 196

4.   Dorian Tunes

a.   Pentatonic or Basically Pentatonic Dorian Tunes

Tune	SH	OSH	NH	Jackson Reference
1. Babe of Bethlehem	78			SF 51, see also AnS 328 "Milton."
2. Jordan's Shore	318	50	177	DE 241
3. Knoxville	140			AnS 296

4. Repose	151			DE 173
5. Royal Band		360		DE 55
6. Villulia		56		SF 21
7. Wondrous Love	252	159	143	SF 88

b. Hexatonic Dorian Tunes with "fa"

1. Sweet Prospect	137	65	DE 197

c. Hexatonic Dorian Tunes with "ti"

1. Blessed Bible		347	DE 49
2. Enquirer		74	SF 87
3. Invocation (2)	193		DE 100
4. Travelling Pilgrim	313	278	DE 293

Note: The tune "Hebrew Children," SH 266, OSH 133, is the nearest to a Phrygian tune that appears in the Jackson lists. It sounds like a major tune ending on the third of the scale, but in both books it is harmonized in minor. The Jackson reference is SF 194.

Appendix II

Tunes using gapped scales count this as one of the characteristics. The others are as follows:

1. Shape; 1a is a modification of this.
2. Form ABB¹A (or its equivalent in a six phrase tune); 2a typical figure repetition in the middle phrases.
3. Typical measure patterns for the metric signature.
4. Mixed meter or rebarring
5. Centonization
6. Refrain

1. IONIAN (MAJOR) TUNES

a. Pentatonic or Basically Pentatonic Ionian Tunes

Tune	SH	OSH	NH	Characteristics
1. Abbeville		33		1, 2a
2. Arnold		285		1, 3
3. Bishop		420		1a, 3, 5
4. Blooming Youth		176		1, 4, 5
5. Burk		92		1, 4, 5
6. Canaan's Land		101		1, 2, 4
7. Columbiana		56		1, 5
8. Cookham	8	81		1, 3
9. Days of Worship		60		1, 2a, 3
10. Dove of Peace	89			1, 3
11. Fleeting Days		348		1, 2a
12. Funeral Thought	257	158	102	1, 3
13. Hallelujah (2)	139			1, 6
14. Happiness	40			1, 3, 5
15. Happy Land		354		1a, 3
16. Happy Sailor		388		3, 6
17. Heavenly Rest		403		1 (for verse), 6
18. I Would See Jesus		75		1, 2a
19. Jackson		317		2a, 4
20. Jewett		105		1, 4, 6
21. Kelley		426		1, 2a, 4
22. Love		303		1, 4
23. Love Divine		30		1, 2a

194

24. Newman		321		1, 2
25. Odem		295		1, 2a, 3
26. Ogletree		138		1, 5
27. Our Journey Home	327			1, 5
28. Pilgrim's Song	106			1, 2a, 5
29. Prospect of Heaven	24			1, 4
30. Rapture	333		123	3, 5
31. Rees		418		1, 2a
32. Restoration (2)		271		1, 5
33. Sharpsburg		39		1, 4
34. Shepherds Rejoice		152		1, 2a
35. Shepherd's Star	310			1, 2a
36. Sidney		437		1, 2a
37. Sing On		381		1, 5
38. Still Better		166		1, 5
39. Struggle On		400		5, 6
40. Timmons		117		1a, 5
41. Vain World Adieu		329		1a, 4
42. Weeping Sinners		108		1, 5
43. Young Convert	308			1, 2a, 5, 6
44. Zion's Light	270			1, 2a

b.   Hexatonic Ionian Tunes with "fa"

1. Aurora			40	1, 3, 4
2. Christian's Conflicts	131			1, 2a, 4
3. Confidence (2)		270		1, 2
4. Corinth		32		2a, 4
5. Holy Army			119	5, 6
6. Immensity	319			1, 2a, 4, 5
7. Indian's Petition	269			1, 2a, 3
8. Invitation (1)	2			1, 2
9. Invocation (1)	72	131		4, 5
10. Land of Pleasure	63			1, 4, 5
11. Loving Kindness (1)			28	1, 2a
12. Marriage in the Skies		438		2a, 5
13. Middlebury	17			1, 3
14. Sacred Rest		435		1a, 3
15. Sufferings of Christ	85			1, 3

c.   Hexatonic Ionian Tunes with "ti"

1. Lindan	168		1, 4
2. Mullins		323	1, 2
(This is "Come Thou Fount," usually called "Nettleton")			
3. O Sing With Me		374	1, 2
4. Parting Friend		414	1, 2, 4
5. Pilgrim's Song	106		1, 2a, 4
6. Return Again		355	1, 4, 5
7. South Union		344	2a, 3
8. Weary Pilgrim's Consolation	298		1, 4

d.   Seven-tone Ionian Tunes

	SH	OSH	NH	Characteristics
1. Derrick	199			1, 2a, 5
2. Intercession	324			1, 4, 5
3. Marion			164	1, 2, 4
4. Newport			17	1, 3, 4
5. Saint's Adieu			124	1, 4, 5
6. Trumpeters	301			1, 2a, 4

2.   AEOLIAN TUNES

a.   Pentatonic or Basically Pentatonic Tunes

Tune	SH	OSH	NH	Characteristics
1. Farewell to All		69		3, 4
2. Happy Christian		399		1a, 3
3. Home				1a, 4
(This has a chorus in the parallel major)				
4. In That Morning	194			1a, 6
5. Parting Friends (1)	35			1, 5
6. Sion's Security			30	1, 2, 3, 4
7. Traveller (1)		108		1, 5

b.   Hexatonic Aeolian Tunes with "ti"

	SH	OSH	NH	Characteristics
1. Babylonian Captivity	164			1, 4·
2. Christian Soldier (3)			120	1a, 3
3. Christian's Nightly Song		416		3, 5
4. Farewell	81			1, 3
5. Friendship		458		1, 2, 5
6. Love the Lord		375		4, 5
7. My Home		51		1, 5
8. Never Turn Back	271	378		1a, 2a
9. New Jerusalem	125			1, 4
10. Northport		324		1, 4, 5
11. Sinner's Friend		132		4, 6
12. Span of Life		379		1, 4

c.   Seven-tone Aeolian Tunes

	SH	OSH	NH	Characteristics
1. Christian's Delight		429		3, 5, 6
2. Delight	102			1a, 3, 5
3. Fellowship		330		1, 2a, 3
4. Georgia	72			1a, 4, 5
5. Worlds Above		315		1, 2a, 5

3.   MIXOLYDIAN TUNES

a.   Pentatonic Tune

	SH	OSH	NH	Characteristics
1. Heavenly Armour	93	129	56	1, 3

Bibliography

a. Books and Articles.

Apel, Willi. *The Harvard Dictionary of Music*. Cambridge: Harvard University Press, 1958 edition.

————. *Gregorian Chant*. Bloomington: Indiana University Press, 1958.

Barbour, J. Murray. *The Church Music of William Billings*. East Lansing: Michigan State University Press, 1960.

Baring-Gould, Sabine. *English Minstrelsie*, Vols. 1–8. Edinburgh: T. C. and E. C. Jack, Grange Publishing Works, 1895.

Baring-Gould, Sabine, and Cecil Sharp. *English Folk-Songs for Schools*. London: J. Curwen and Sons, Ltd. No date.

Baring-Gould, S., and H. Fleetwood Sheppard. *A Garland of Country Song*. London: Methuen and Co., 1905.

Baring-Gould, S., H. Fleetwood Sheppard, and F. W. Bussell. *Songs of the West*. London: Methuen and Co., 1905.

Barrett, W. A. *Standard English Songs*. Bks. 1–5. London: Augener and Co., 1890.

Bayard, Samuel Preston. *Hill Country Tunes: Instrumental Folk Music of Southwestern Pennsylvania*. Philadelphia: American Folklore Society, 1944.

Broadwood, Lucy E. *English Traditional Songs and Carols*. London: Boosey and Co., 1908.

Broadwood, Lucy E., and J. A. Fuller Maitland. *English Country Songs*. London: The Leadenhall Press, 1893.

Bronson, Bertrand. *Traditional Tunes of the Child Ballads*, 2 vols. Princeton: Princeton University Press, 1959.

Brown, Theron, and Hezekiah Butterworth. *The Story of the Hymns and Tunes*. Chicago: W. P. Blessing and Co., 1906. (Cited in notes as Butterworth-Brown.)

Buchanan, Annabel Morris. *Folk Hymns of America*. New York: J. Fischer and Brother, 1938.

Cartwright, Peter. *Autobiography of Peter Cartwright*. Nashville, Tenn.: Abingdon Press, 1956.

Chappell, W. *A Collection of National English Airs*. London: Chappell and Co., 1838.

————. *Popular Music of the Olden Time*. Vols. 1 and 2. London: Chappell and Co., 1855–59.

Chase, Gilbert. *America's Music*. New York: McGraw-Hill Book Co., Inc., 1955.

Davis, Arthur Kyle. *Traditional Ballads of Virginia*. Cambridge: Harvard University Press, 1929.

Dearmer, Percy, R. Vaughan Williams, and Martin Shaw. *The Oxford Book of Carols*. London: Oxford University Press, 1928.

Eskew, Harry. *The Life and Work of William Walker*. Master's thesis, New Orleans Baptist Theological Seminary, 1960.

Foote, Henry Wilder. *Three Centuries of American Hymnody*. Cambridge: Harvard University Press, 1940.

Fisher, William Arms. *Ye Olde New England Psalm Tunes*. Boston: Oliver Ditson, 1930.

Greig, Gavin, and Alexander Keith. *Last Leaves of Traditional Ballads and Ballad Airs*. Aberdeen: The Buchan Club, 1925.

Hamm, Charles, "The Chapins and Sacred Music in the South and West." *Journal of Research in Music Education*, viii, 2 (Fall, 1960).

Howard, John Tasker. *Our American Music*. New York: Thomas Y. Crowell Co., 1931. Two subsequent editions.

Jackson, George Pullen. *Another Sheaf of White Spirituals*. Gainesville: University of Florida Press, 1952.

———. *Down East Spirituals and Others*. New York: J. J. Augustin, 1943.

———. *Spiritual Folk-Songs of Early America*. New York: J. J. Augustin, 1937.

———. *White Spirituals in the Southern Uplands*. Chapel Hill: University of North Carolina Press, 1933.

Johnson, Charles A. *The Frontier Campmeeting: Religion's Harvest Time*. Dallas, Tex.: Southern Methodist University Press, 1955.

Johnson, Helen Kendrick. *Our Familiar Songs and Who Made Them*. New York: H. Holt and Co., 1901.

Journal of the Folk-Song Society. London: The Folk-Song Society. All volumes, beginning 1898.

Kidson, Frank. *Traditional Tunes*. Oxford: Charles Taphouse and Son, 1891.

Lightwood, James T. *Methodist Music in the Eighteenth Century*. London: The Epworth Press, J. Alfred Sharp, 1927.

Lowens, Irving. "John Wyeth's *Repository of Sacred Music*, Part Second: a Northern Precursor of Southern Folk Hymnody." *Journal of the American Musicological Society*, v, 2 (1952).

McCutchan, Robert Guy. *Hymn Tune Names*. New York and Nashville: The Abingdon Press, 1957.

Metcalf, Frank J. *American Writers and Compilers of Sacred Music*. New York and Cincinnati: The Abingdon Press, 1928.

———. "The Easy Instructor." *The Musical Quarterly*, xxiii (1937), 89–97.

———. *Stories of Hymn Tunes*. New York and Cincinnati: The Abingdon Press, 1928.

Miller, Perry. *Jonathan Edwards*. New York: W. Sloane Associates, 1949.

Motherwell, William. *Minstrelsy, Ancient and Modern*. Glasgow: John Wylie, 1873.

Ninde, Edward S. *The Story of the American Hymn*. New York and Cincinnati: The Abingdon Press, 1926.

Parkes, Henry Bamford. *Jonathan Edwards, the Fiery Puritan*. New York: Minton, Balch and Co., 1930.

Patrick, Millar. *Four Centuries of Scottish Psalmody*. London, Glasgow: The Oxford University Press, 1949.

Petrie, George. *The Complete Collection of Irish Music*, edited by Charles Villiers Stanford. London: Boosey and Co., 1902–5.

Reese, Gustave. *Music in the Middle Ages*. New York: W. W. Norton and Co., 1940.

Sharp, Cecil J. *Country Dance Tunes*. 11 sets. London: Novello and Co. Ltd., 1902–22.

———. *English Folk Songs from the Southern Appalachians*. 2 vols. Edited by Maud Karpeles. London: Oxford University Press, Humphrey Milford, 1932.

———. *English Folk-Song: Some Conclusions*. 2d ed. London: Novello and Co. Ltd., 1936.

———. *Folk-Song Airs*. Collected and arranged for the pianoforte. Bks. 1–3. London: Novello and Co. Ltd., 1908.

————. *Folk-Songs from Somerset*. Series 1–5. London: Simpkins and Co. Ltd., 1909.

Stevenson, Arthur Linwood. *The Story of Southern Hymnology*. Roanoke, Va.: published by the author, 1931.

Stokoe, John. *Northumbrian Minstrelsy*. Newcastle-on-Tyne: The Society of Antiquarians, 1882.

————. *Songs and Ballads of Northern England*. Newcastle-on-Tyne and London: Walter Scott Ltd., 1899.

Terry, Richard Runciman. *A Forgotten Psalter and Other Essays*. London: Oxford University Press, 1929.

Trollope, Mrs. Frances. *Domestic Manners of the Americans*. New York: Vintage Books, 1960.

Tye, Christopher. *The Actes of the Apostles*. Manuscript copy, 1553.

Sweet, William Warren. *Religion in Colonial America*. New York: Charles Scribners' Sons, 1951.

————. *Religion in the Development of American Culture, 1765–1840*. New York: Scribner, 1952.

Yasser, Joseph. *A Theory of Evolving Tonality*. New York: American Library of Musicology, 1932.

————. *Medieval Quartal Harmony: a Plea for Restoration*. New York: American Library of Musicology, 1938.

b.   Hymnals and Singing School Manuals.

Adgate, Andrew. *Rudiments of Music*. 8th ed. Philadelphia: Matthew Carey, 1803.

Adgate, Andrew and Spicer. *Philadelphia Harmony, Pt. II*. Philadelphia, 1790.

Aiken, J. B. *The Christian Minstrel*. Philadelphia, 1850 and 1856 editions.

Atwill, T. H. *New York Collection of Sacred Harmony*. Title page missing, 1794.

Baptist Hymnals: *The Baptist Hymnal*. Philadelphia: The American Baptist Publication Society, 1883.

Baptist Hymnals: *The Baptist Hymn and Praise Book*. Nashville, Tenn.: The Sunday School Board of the Southern Baptist Convention, 1904.

————. *The Baptist Hymn and Tune Book*. Title page missing, 1875.

————. *The Service of Song for Baptist Churches*. Boston: Gould and Lincoln, 1872.

Bayley, Daniel. *The Essex Harmony*. Newbury Port, 1771.

Belcher, Supply. *The Harmony of Maine*. Boston, 1794.

Belknap, Daniel. *The Evangelical Harmony*. Boston, 1800.

Benham, Asahel. *Social Harmony*. New Haven, 1798.

Billings, William. *The Continental Harmony*. Boston, 1794.

————. *The New England Psalm Singer*. Boston, 1770.

————. *The Singing Master's Assistant*. Boston, 1778.

————. *The Suffolk Harmony*. Boston, 1786.

Bradbury, William B. *The Devotional Hymn and Tune Book*. Philadelphia: The American Baptist Publication Society, 1864.

————. *The Jubilee*. Boston, 1858.

————. *The Victory*. New York, 1889.

Brownson, Oliver. *Select Harmony*. Title page missing, 1783.

Bull, Amos. *The Responsary*. Worcester, Mass., 1795.

Caldwell, William. *The Union Harmony or Family Musician*. Maryville, Tenn., 1837.

Carden, Allen D. *The Missouri Harmony*. Cincinnati, 1838.

Christian Church. *Psalms and Hymns and Spiritual Songs*. New York, 1875.

Collins, T. K. jr. *Timbrel of Zion.* Philadelphia, 1854.

Comnuck, Thomas. *Indian Melodies,* harmonized by T. Hastings. New York: G. Lane and C. B. Tippell for the M. E. Church, 1845.

Congregational Church. *Congregational Hymn and Tune Book.* New Haven: Darrie and Peck for the General Association, 1856.

Davisson, Ananias. *Supplement to the Kentucky Harmony.* 3rd ed. Harrisonburg, Va., 1825.

Dickerson, John jr. *The Musical Instructor.* Philadelphia, 1818.

Dyer, Samuel. *The Philadelphia Selection of Sacred Music.* 4th ed. New York: printed for the author, c. 1828.

Fargo, G. W., and Jesse Pierce. *Ancient Harmony Revived.* 3rd ed. Boston: Perkins and Whipple, 1850.

Fillmore, A. D. *Harp of Zion.* Cincinnati: R. W. Carroll and Co., 1867.

Fillmore, James Henry. *New Christian Hymn and Tune Book.* Cincinnati: Fillmore Bros., 1882 and 1887.

Fobes, Azariah. *The Delaware Harmony.* Philadelphia, 1809.

French, Jacob. *The Psalmodist's Companion.* Worcester, Mass., 1793.

Funk, Joseph. *Choral Music.* Harrisonburg, Rockingham Co., Va., 1816.

————. *Genuine Church Music.* Winchester, Va., 1832.

Hauser, William. *The Hesperian Harp.* Philadelphia: T. K. and P. G. Collins, 1848.

Hayden, A. S. *The Sacred Melodeon.* Philadelphia: T. K. and P. G. Collins, 1849.

Hickock, J. H., and George Fleming. *Evangelical Musick.* Harrisburg, Pa., 1834.

Hillman, Joseph. *The Revivalist.* Troy and Albany, N.Y., 1868 and 1872 revisions.

Holden, Oliver. *American Harmony.* Boston: Thomas and Andrews, 1793.

————. *Union Harmony.* Boston: Thomas and Andrews, 1793.

————. *Worcester Collection of Sacred Harmony.* 8th ed. Boston: Thomas and Andrews, 1803.

Holyoke, Samuel. *The Christian Harmonist* (For Baptist Churches). Salem, Mass.: J. Cushing, 1804.

————. *Columbian Repository of Sacred Harmony.* Exeter, N.H.: Henry Ranlet, 1805 (?).

Ingalls, Jeremiah. *Christian Harmony or Songster's Companion.* Exeter, N.H., 1805.

Jackson, John. B. *Knoxville Harmony.* Pumpkintown, E. Tenn., 1840.

Jenks, Stephen. *New England Harmonist.* Title page missing, 1799.

————. *The Musical Harmonist.* Title page missing, 1800.

Johnson, Andrew W. *The Western Psalmodist.* Nashville, Tenn., 1853.

Jones, Darius E. *Temple Melodies.* New York: Mason and Law, 1852.

Kimball, Jacob jr. *Rural Harmony.* Boston, 1793.

Kirk, Edward N. *Songs for Social and Public Worship.* Boston: Hoyt, 1867.

Law, Andrew. *The Art of Singing.* 4th ed. Cambridge, Mass., 1803.

————. *Christian Harmony.* Windsor, Vt., 1805.

————. *Rudiments of Music.* 4th ed. Cheshire, Conn., 1792.

Leavitt, Joshua. *The Christian Lyre.* New York, 1830.

Lewis, Freeman. *Beauties of Harmony.* Pittsburgh, 1814.

————. *Songs of Zion.* Pittsburgh, 1824.

Little, William, and William Smith. *The Easy Instructor.* Albany, N.Y., 1802 (?).

Lyon, James. *Urania.* Philadelphia, 1761.

Mansfield, D. H. *The American Vocalist.* Boston: W. J. Reynolds and Co., 1849 and 1869 revised editions.

Mason, Lowell. *The Choir or Union Collection of Church Music.* 9th ed. Boston, 1839.

Methodist Hymnals, etc. *The Harmonist.* New York: T. Mason for the Methodist Episcopal Church, 1837.

————. *Hymnal of the Methodist Episcopal Church.* Cincinnati, 1886. Commissioned by the General Conference of 1876.

————. *The Methodist Collection of Hymns and Tunes.* New York: Carlton and Porter for the M. E. Church, 1849.

————. *The Methodist Harmonist.* 2nd ed. New York: T. Mason, 1833.

————. *The Methodist Hymnal.* Nashville, Tenn., and Dallas, Tex.: Publishing House of the Methodist Episcopal Church, South, 1905.

————. *New Hymn and Tune Book.* New York: The Methodist Episcopal Church, 1867.

Nettleton, Asahel. *Village Hymns.* New York, 1828.

————. *Zion's Harp.* New Haven: N. and S. S. Jocelyn, 1824.

New Jersey Harmony. Philadelphia: John McCulloch, 1797.

O'Kane, T. C. *Jasper and Gold.* Cincinnati: Hitchcock and Walden, 1877.

Old Hundred Collection of Sacred Music. Boston, 1824.

Perkins, T. E. *Sacred Lute.* New York: F. J. Huntington, 1864.

Presbyterian Hymnals, etc. *Book of Hymns and Tunes.* Richmond, Va.: Presbyterian Committee of Publication for the Presbyterian Church in the U.S., 1874.

————. *The Hymnal.* Philadelphia: The Presbyterian Board of Publication and Sabbath School Work, 1919.

————. *Hymnal of the Presbyterian Church.* Philadelphia: Presbyterian Board of Publication, 1867.

————. *The Presbyterian Psalmodist,* Thomas Hastings, editor. Philadelphia: Presbyterian Board of Publication, 1851.

Read, Daniel. *American Singing Book.* New Haven, 1785.

————. *The Columbian Harmonist.* Dedham, Mass.: H. Mann, 1806.

Rhinehart, William. *The American or Union Harmonist.* Chambersburg, Pa., 1831.

Robinson, Charles S. *Laudes Domini.* New York: The Century Co., 1890.

————. *A Selection of Spiritual Songs.* New York: The Century Co., 1881.

————. *Social Hymns and Tunes.* Cincinnati, 1863.

Sacred Songs for Family and Social Worship. New York: The American Tract Society, 1842.

Sankey, Ira D., James McGranahan, and George C. Stebbins. *Christian Endeavor Edition of Gospel Hymns No. 6.* Boston: United Society of Christian Endeavor, 1891.

Shumway, Nehemiah. *The American Harmony.* Title page missing, 1793.

Smith, Henry. *The Church Harmony.* 21st ed. Chambersburg, Pa., 1841.

Swan, M. L. *New Harp of Columbia.* (Reprint of 1867 edition). Nashville, Tenn.: Publishing House of the M. E. Church, South, 1921.

Swan, Timothy. *New England Harmony.* Northampton, Mass.: Andrew Wright, 1801.

Tans'ur, William. *American Harmony.* Newbury Port: Daniel Bayley, 1771.

————. *Compleat Melody.* London: Robert Brown, 1736.

————. *Royal Melody Compleat.* London, 1764.

Village Harmony, or New England Repository of Sacred Music. 15th ed. Probably compiled by Charles Norris. Exeter, 1818.

Walker, William. *The Christian Harmony.* Rev. ed. Philadelphia: Miller's Bible and Publishing House, 1875.

————. *The Southern Harmony and Musical Companion.* New York: Hastings House, 1939.

Wakefield, Samuel. *The Christian's Harp.* Pittsburgh, 1837.

Wenger, Martin D. *The Philharmonia*. Elkhart, Ind.: Menonite Publishing Co., 1875.

Western Lyre. Cincinnati: W. B. Snyder and W. L. Chappell, 1823.

White, B. F., and E. J. King. *Original Sacred Harp* (Denson Revision). Haleyville, Ala.: Sacred Harp Publishing Co., 1936.

Woodbury, I. B. *Harp of the South*. New York: Mason and Law, 1853.

Wyeth, John. *Repository of Sacred Music*. Harrisburg, Pa.: 1810.

―――. *Repository of Sacred Music, Part II*. 2d ed. Harrisburg, Pa., 1820.

Index of Tunes

1. References following an "M" refer to page numbers of musical examples.
2. In a few instances a tune is referred to, as a quotation from a table of contents, by a name different from that in any of the three books. These names are marked with an asterisk, references are given, and a cross-reference is provided.
3. Since it is impossible to provide cross-references for all names by which a tune is known, only those alternative names used in the text are given, with their references. For other names, use the lists on pages 146–56 and 164–77.
4. No attempt has been made to give modifications in this index other than in the case of the musical examples.

203

Index

TO ME OF

"...the Spirit."—1

alled   to   die,
nar - ble brow,
dy - ing face,

SING TO

ong   be - gin,
lown   to rest,
hose   I   love,

C., 1810, and died
dler. She wrote
n in 1840 was on
wrote the melod

sweet   song
me   down
h - ble   those

She first married Mr. Dana, and afterwards became Mrs. Shindler
husband, "I Am a Pilgrim and a Stranger." The hymn written in
Prof. John Massengale, some time between 1860 and 1869, wro
Harp and other books. Alto by S. M. Denson, 1911.